The Children from Monkey Island

Dedicated to our uncle George Herbert Burton.

Copyright © 2015, 2016, 2021 and 2024 Clive Tester.
Published by Clive Tester. First edition December 2015. Second edition April 2016 with additions made August 2016. Centenary edition May 2021 with additions March 2024. Amazon edition April 2024.

All rights reserved. No part of this publication may be reproduced, stored in a retrieval system, or transmitted in any form, or by any means, electronic, mechanical, photocopying or otherwise, without prior permission from the author, his representative, heirs or beneficiaries. Permission is granted for the author's representative, heirs and beneficiaries to re-publish this book. Permission is granted for the use of brief quotations in a book review written for inclusion in a newspaper, magazine, broadcast etc.

CONTENTS

Acknowledgements	1
Introduction	2
Citations	3
The Vernacular of Under the Hill	4
Prologue: Monkey Island and the Crystal	5
Chapter 1: The Days of Monkey Island	7
Chapter 2: The Days of "The Mud 'Ole"	40
Chapter 3: The Days of the Alpha	68
Chapter 4: The Days of Chalk and Dragonflies	86
Chapter 5: The Days of Change	145
Epilogue: The View from the 21st Century	153
Appendix A: The Lime Kiln of Pickles Way	154
Appendix B: Layer, Peldon and the Alpha Railways	155
Appendix C: "Ham, Spam or Jam". Memories of the Alpha	164
Appendix D: A Swallow Falls Over Egypt Bay. The DH108 air crash	167

Cover picture: Children swimming to Monkey Island at Cliffe Creek in the early years of the 1900s with the kilns at the mouth of the creek in the background.
Painting copyright Richard Bizley 2014.

Sunset photograph at the end of the Prologue on page 6: The Dry Digger Lake. Photograph by Clive Tester 1991.

A Winter's day in the Picnic Grounds Chapter 4 page 136: Photograph by Clive Tester 1991.

The photographs by Bob Knight on pages 85, 87, 88, 89, 110 and 114 were digitally colourised by Bob Knight from original black and white photographs.

ACKNOWLEDGEMENTS

I would like to thank the following people for their help and contributions to this book:

My mother Gwen for priceless memories and insights and for proof reading. My son Richard for proof reading. My wife Frila for her support in providing me the time to write this book and my son John Mark for his patience the many times I was busy with writing and for spell checking later editions.

My extended family.

My thanks to Philip MacDougall, Terry Pauline and Hayley Springhall, Peter and Rita Carey, Don and Angela Moore, Penelope Harris nee Pennell, David Willis, Richard Bizley, Peter Knight, Pastor James Ebbs, David West, Douglas Arnold, Wendy Meader, Donna and Alan Smith, Ian Pearson, Don and Ross Pople, Dr. Roger Simmonds, Andrew Blackwell, Bob Knight, Terry Hoare, Paul Scott, Catherine Groves, Teri Collins, Caroline Chalice, Patrick Morrison, Sally Ann Hodd, Evro Dockwray, Nigel Springhall, Gordon Edgar, Tony Millatt, Vivienne and Kevin Duvall, Joy Daniels and Andrea Kennard. My gratitude to our good friends Stuart and Sally Hall for their support.

Thanks posthumously to Sis and Burt Hoare, George Slater, Eddie Burton, Sid Burton, John and Gwen Burton, Victor Tester Senior, Jack Sullivan, Perce Springhall, Percy Payne and Herbert Weber.

Thanks too for:

Clifford "Dick" and Pauline Dowsett, and Stan and Doris Beeching for information and memories and for proof reading chapters 1 to 3. To Stan Doris and Malcolm Beeching for entertaining us at their home. Eric Slater for sharing his memories of the Alpha with me over the years. Andy and Janet Keats for proof reading and information. Ken and Carol Baxter and Pauline Springhall for entertaining us at Boatwick House and providing us with photographs and many memories. David Green and Daniel Wilmer-Brown of the Cliffe at Hoo Historical Society and members of the Cliffe at Hoo Historical Society for providing me with information and advice for this book. Gill Moore for facilitating local events where I had the opportunity to meet the people of the Cliffe cement industry. Dylan Moore for his contributions to chapter 1 via e-mail correspondence where cited. Thanks to Claire Seymour and the Amberley Museum & Heritage Centre for the information and photographs of Peldon.

Thanks to my old school friends: Posthumously to Paul Enticknap for his words of support and encouragement. To Adrian Hatcher for his extensive photographic survey of Under the Hill in 2015 and to David Arnold for his words of support and information for this project. To Shaun and Barry Hutchings for championing this book.

My gratitude is extended to the staff of Blue Circle who during my boyhood provided me with information on their industry and provided me with visits to their factories and quarries in the Medway area. My gratitude to Blue Circle and the Port of London Authority for granting me access to their lands around Cliffe in the 1980s and 1990s to take photographs.

My thanks to the British Geological Survey and the Kent Messenger for allowing me to use their photographs in this book and to the Ordnance Survey for their assistance.

Thanks to Paul Rhodes and LEFA Print for their help and support with earlier editions.

My thanks to all who have contributed with their memories photographs and support.

INTRODUCTION TO THE CENTENARY EDITION

It was a week before Christmas 2015 when The Children from Monkey Island was first published and since that time many friends have come forward with additional information and photographs that have been augmented into this edition. And it is fitting that this new edition comes in the year 2021: one hundred years after the closure of two great factories that shaped the landscape of our village. 1921 saw the closure of the Curtis's and Harvey munitions works at Lower Hope Point and the Victorian era cement works in the Francis Chalk Quarry.

To be a child of Cliffe in the 20th century was a privilege of a rare kind. Our childhood was gifted with a sense of freedom born of a place that we all knew as Under the Hill: that was our term for the quarries and marshlands that lay beyond Pond Hill at Cliffe. For us, a sense of splendid isolation prevailed in that land which lay between our village and the banks of a river that flows wide and fast. To us it was a place of peace and reflection. There too was to be found an alluring sense of wonder and adventure among the ghostly relics of the industries that had shaped that landscape. The landscape of Under the Hill is so closely entwined with the history of our local industries that it must play an essential part in this book. For the cement industry of Cliffe has left us with a valuable legacy of wetlands and wooded quarries the spirit of which I endeavour to convey through the memories of those who once lived, worked and played Under the Hill. And to that purpose I have, by writing in the first person, endeavoured to express something of my own experience of this land. And to that end too I have used the vernacular of Cliffe throughout this book.

In the time since its first publication some of those who helped with and championed this book have sadly passed away. I would like to pay tribute to those good people: my mother Gwen and my brother Eric, Stan and Doris Beeching, Gill Moore, Pauline Dowsett, Don Pople, Eric Slater, Evro Dockwray, Peter Carey and our great friend Paul Enticknap.

Finally, I would like to express my gratitude to those many people who have been so encouraging toward The Children from Monkey Island.

Clive Tester May 2021.

A place of peace and reflection. Cliffe Marshes from Allens Hill.
Photograph by Clive Tester February 1991.

CITATIONS

1: Mildred Hoare AKA Aunt Sis. 1901- 1992.
2: Sid Burton 1916 - 2013.
3: My mother, Gwen Tester nee Burton b 1927.
5: Eric Slater. Pontoon crane operator, b 1927.
6: Victor Edward Tester b 1950
7: Dylan Moore. www.cementkilns.co.uk
8: The Cement Industry 1796-1914: A History. Major A J Francis 1977 ISBN 0 7153 7386 2.
9: Register of air raids and alarms held at the Medway Archives Office reference: SRDC_582.
10: Jack Sullivan 1910 - 2002. Engineer at the Alpha.
11: Clifford "Dick" Dowsett. Pontoon crane operator, b. 1929.
12: Victor Albert Tester. 1927-2007. (Victor Tester Senior)
13. Terry Springhall.
14. Stan Beeching. B. 1916. Worked at the Alpha in a number of roles.
15. The Cement Railways of Kent. B,D Stoyel and R.W Kidner. Oakwood Press 1973. ISBN 0 85361 370 2.
16. Stella Holroyd, nee Tester.
17. Steve Holroyd.
18. Isle of Grain Railways. Locomotion paper number seventy-seven. Adrian Gray. Oakwood Press 1974.
19. The Hoo Peninsula. Philip MacDougall. John Hallewell Publications 1980. ISBN 0 905540 19 0.
20. Jim Preston's RSPB commissioned report via Cliffe at Hoo Historical Society.
21. Historic Environment Desk-Based Assessment. Cliffe Pools RSPB reserve. NGR572000 177000. Report number 2007094. Project number 3126. By Richard James, with contributions from Jim Preston & Victor Smith. Commissioned by the RSPB.
22. Clive Tester.
23. Steve Martin.
24. English Heritage Research Department Report Series 011-2011, Curtis's and Harvey Ltd Explosives Factory Cliffe and Cliffe Woods Medway. Pullen, Newsome, Williams and Cocroft.
25. Via Dave Green of the Cliffe at Hoo Historical Society: Chatham, Rochester and Gillingham News Saturday, February 27, 1904. The Cliffe Explosions. Inquest at Rochester & Cliffe. **25A:** Via Dave Green at www.cliffehistory.co.uk.
26. David Arnold.
27. Penelope Harris nee Pennell.
28. Ken Baxter.
29. Clifford Tester b 1959
30. Marshall, Arthur, Dictionary of Explosives, 1920.
31. Perce Springhall.
32. Eric Tester b 1957.
33. Adrian Hatcher b 1965.
34. Don Moore.
35. Andy and Janet Keats.
36. Winifred Brenchley Nee Higglesden.
37. Ian Pearson.

THE VERNACULAR OF UNDER THE HILL

Under the Hill: Of Cliffe folklore; Cliffe Marshes and the chalk quarries that lay beyond Pond Hill. It is a term that has been in use from at least as far back as the early 1930s[3].

Mud Hole: A clay pit. During the late 19th century and early 20th century the clay pits at Cliffe were hand dug by muddies.

Muddies: Men who specialised in manual clay digging before the introduction of mechanical methods. This was a term in wider use in North Kent.

The Track: The Francis Chalk Quarry was known as the Track from its first use for motorcycling from 1962.

The Alpha: Throughout this book the term the Alpha is used to refer to the cement factory at Salt Lane. Built between 1910 and 1913[1] by the Thames Portland Cement Co. Ltd its ownership changed to The Alpha Cement Company in 1934[15]. In 1938 the Alpha Group was taken over jointly by the APCM and Tunnel Cement, and wholly by the APCM in 1948[15]. As far as operations at the factory were concerned the factory remained within the remit of the Alpha until the early 1950s[14]. *The Alpha* as a term for the Salt Lane cement works and its associated quarries has remained firmly within the village vernacular to this day. Until recent times the reception building at the entrance to the site remained. The building bore upon a stone plaque the words: Thames Portland Cement Co Ltd 1913. In its earlier years the Salt Lane factory was known locally as the New Factory[1]. More details of the ownership changes to the factory can be found in chapter 3.

The wetlands and wooded quarries of Under the Hill. Photograph by Frila Tester March 2017.

PROLOGUE

MONKEY ISLAND AND THE CRYSTAL:

TWO HOT SUMMERS 1911 AND 1976

The path to the Crystal. Photograph by Clive Tester 1985.

In 1911 the path that is shown in this photograph was an industrial railway line that linked the Francis Chalk Quarry to Cliffe Creek. At Cliffe Creek lived a community built around the cement industry. In that small community lay the house of the Slater family of whom the daughter Mildred became known to my generation as Aunt Sis. In the Slater household Mr Slater oftentimes played accordion for his family's entertainment while dancing back to back with Mrs Slater. The garden of the Slater household sometimes flooded on high tides as water overflowed from the adjacent Cliffe Creek. I am told that 1911 was a hot summer. And in that summer the ten-year-old Aunt Sis and her friends spent their time swimming in Cliffe Creek. They often swam out to a small island in the middle of the creek. Aunt Sis told me that the adults referred to that island as Monkey Island: the boisterous children who played there were "little monkeys" (Citation: Aunt Sis 1901-1992).

Sixty-five years later came a monumental hot summer that marked my transition from junior school to secondary school. 1976 was the summer of my 11th birthday. My family, friends and I spent most of that summer swimming in a lake close to Cliffe Creek. The lake spans the southern border of the path in the photograph, and we knew the lake as the Crystal: In those days, the newly dug lakes retained clear clean water. The summer of 1976 was so hot that I recalled never once feeling cold through the hours that we spent in that water. And as we swam, cattle often grazed placidly in the meadows around the lake. In the Crystal there were a couple of artefacts left over from the days of the Alpha:

There was a flat-bottomed boat of heavy wooden construction that had likely been used to provide access to the floating pontoon cranes back in their day. I recall that it was large enough to accommodate five or six of us children. We would float out in the boat, then sway in unison such that water began to fill the boat. We would sit in the water filled boat as it drifted wherever the breeze took us while the hot summer sun of '76 warmed the confined water to a bath like temperature. Sometimes we'd see a water vole swimming near the clay banks of the lake. Eventually we would bail the water out of the boat with our hands. We would often find a stickleback or two in the water filled boat.

Another curiosity was a pontoon float that had long become detached from its crane. It was a riveted iron cylinder around six feet in diameter and around 20 feet in length. We would clamber onto its sun-baked top: it was almost too hot to stand on it with our bare feet. We would set it in rotation by running on the spot; it rolled with increasing speed until one by one we fell into the water.

That floating piece of ironwork fascinated me for it was representative of the big engineering that lay all around us: the big engineering characterised by the sunken pontoon cranes and the long-forgotten railway lines the sleepers of which lay part buried in the path to the Crystal. It was of the big engineering embodied in the Alpha with its towering chimneys and cavernous silos that was ever present in our landscape and now all quiescent. It was of the big engineering that had shaped the land to which I would develop a special connection: those vast and mysterious quarries born of the big engineering that possessed the power to inspire.

For me too, these things represented a poignant symbol of days of old and of the memories that were passed on to me by the folk who once made a living there. Good people like Bert and Sis Hoare. Bert Hoare operated the pontoon cranes that gave us our childhood places like the Crystal. Bert witnessed at close hand the flood of that century: back in 1953 he was operating a pontoon crane when he observed water cascading over the sea wall from the tidal surge that flooded part of the marshes.

On our ways back from our days swimming, in those sultry evenings of 1976, we would sometimes drop in on Bert and Sis at Quarry Cottages for a glass of water to slake our thirst. We were always welcome.

All our thanks and appreciation to Bert Hoare (1899 to 1978) and to Mildred "Aunt Sis" Hoare (1901 to 1992).

CHAPTER 1

THE DAYS OF MONKEY ISLAND:

AUNT SIS OF THE EARLY 1900s

In my boyhood years in the 1970s, the very essence of Under the Hill was of a special tranquillity and permanence. The landscape of my youth seemed reassuringly unchanging and far removed from the complexities of the world. But hidden among the hawthorn and bramble bushes were relics that offered curious glimpses into this landscape's past. They spoke of a time when Under the Hill was a place where folk once lived and worked, and of a landscape that was dynamic and ever changing. In the 1970s, I was privileged to befriend someone who had lived and worked at the time when the marshes were still yielding to the industrial revolution: Mildred Hoare nee Slater AKA Aunt Sis who told me much of Cliffe Marshes of old. Let us take a glimpse into the home and the wider landscape of Aunt Sis' childhood of the Edwardian era:

The Slater family lived in one of two cottages at the mouth of the creek; the house was black in colour[2]. Mr William Slater was Foreman at Cliffe Creek and was known as Tubby. He had joined the Navy at an early age and later came to Cliffe *via* the Navy [1&2]. Aunt Sis recalled to me how her father smoked a clay pipe of the type with a long curved stem. Often the young Aunt Sis ran an errand to buy goods from the village and among them tobacco for her father's pipe. There were many different brands of tobacco available, and Mr Slater would often vary his brand. One brand in particular consisted of a twist of compressed tobacco that Mr Slater would whittle into flakes with a penknife into his pipe. While out working around marshes and the sea wall the men wore long coats the inside pockets of which accommodated several of these long pipes. If one of these fragile pipes got broken, as they often did, it would be discarded and another pulled out from the coat.

I found this clay pipe in the mudflats of Lower Hope Point. It is of the type that Aunt Sis described her father as smoking: who knows, this might even be one of Tubby Slater's old pipes.

As night fell over Cliffe Creek oil lamps lit the Slater household, and across the darkening marshes to the east a solitary light blazed upon the distant horizon. In this period, a light ship was stationed at the mouth of the Thames off of Southend. As evening progressed, the coal fire would burn down to a pile of brightly glowing embers. Oftentimes a smoke-jaded clay pipe, darkly stained with malodorous tar, would be placed among that radiant mass within the hearth. Come morning, fresh as new, a stainless white pipe would emerge from the cinders.

The Slater household was located among the Victorian era cement works at the mouth of the creek[1] close to the set of bottle kilns shown in the pictures below. Francis and Company established the cement works at this site in the late 1860s[7&19]. The site was known as The Nine Elms[1 & 7]. The bank of nine kilns shown on the photographs below were the first to be built by Francis on this site. A further ten kilns were added to the site by 1886[7]. Cement production from the works at the mouth of the creek formerly ceased around 1900[7]. For a period of time following the cessation of cement production at this site lime was burned in the kilns of the original bank of nine, as recalled by Aunt Sis. Lime production in these kilns had ceased sometime before 1920.

With the cessation of cement production, the Nine Elms plant was turned over to the production of whiting[7] and the ordnance survey maps of this time reflect the change: an 1897 map describes the works at the mouth of the creek as cement works; the 1908 edition shows the factory as a whiting works. Whiting is ground chalk that has been size graded via a settling process. The old slurry backs of the Nine Elms cement plant were probably used to settle chalk slurry in their new role in the production of whiting[7]. In the settling process, the finer chalk particles that remain at the top of the slurry back are drawn off and dried[7]. Whiting production at the site continued into the 1930s[7].

Left: The original bank of nine Victorian era bottle kilns at the mouth of Cliffe Creek. Note the Coastguard Cottages in the background. Photograph by Clive Tester April 1983.

Below: Monkey Island at Cliffe Creek in the early years of the 1900s with the kilns at the mouth of the creek in the background. Painting copyright Richard Bizley 2014.

The Cliffe Creek bottle kilns. Photographs by Adrian Hatcher 2015.

The Cliffe Creek bottles kilns. Photograph by Clive Tester 2015.

Interior of the Cliffe Creek bottle kilns. Photograph by Adrian Hatcher 2015.

Aunt Sis recalled to me a story that lived in the lore of the area: in the early years of the operation of the bottle kilns at the mouth of Cliffe Creek smoke from their low chimneys often drifted over the adjacent Cliffe Fort. That was until General Gordon expressed concern for the health of the soldiers at the fort. Hence the addition of the wonderful iron chimney arrangement shown in the cover picture of this book.

In the early 1900s, there existed a railway network linking the Cliffe Creek works with its source of chalk at the Francis Chalk Quarry a mile to the east. This railway network also served to bring coal despatched from wharfs on the Thames to cement kilns that were located within the Francis Chalk Quarry. Adrian Gray's book[18] provides comprehensive details of the railway system: The railway was constructed after the re building of the Cliffe Creek works in the early 1870s to a gauge 3' 8½". Aveling and Chaplin locomotives operated on the network. The railway superseded an earlier and more sedate form of transport at the site. Prior to the railway, materials transport from the Francis Chalk Quarry to Cliffe Creek was via a canal that ran adjacent to Creek Road.

AUNT SIS' WALK TO SCHOOL: A JOURNEY THROUGH AN INDUSTRIAL LANDSCAPE

Aunt Sis attended school at the Buttway Cliffe, and walked from Cliffe Creek to school daily with her school friends. Their route to school took them from their home at the mouth of the creek and past the cement works at the eastern inland end of the creek. Here I.C Johnson had established the first cement works at Cliffe in 1853[19], and operations at this site ceased in 1886[7]. In the days of Aunt Sis' childhood, near to this location stood the Canal Tavern known as "the Shant"[1]. Near to the creek also stood two houses in this period: Chalk House, which was built from blocks of chalk[1], and Ivy House[1]. Onto the jagged flint of Creek Road they proceeded toward the direction of yet another complex of cement kilns a little less than a mile to the east: these stood before the cliffs of the Francis Chalk Quarry. A railway line followed Creek Road closely. The line lay to the south of Creek Road on the bank of the former canal. An iron grating that was associated with the operation of the old canal survived into the 1970s; it was located near to Cliffe Creek in what might have been a sluice[1].

THE FIRST MUD HOLE

After a walk of around 10 minutes, Aunt Sis and her friends approached the eastern end of Creek Road and neared the first of two clay pits that were used to supply clay to the cement works that existed in the Francis Chalk Quarry nearby to the east. These were known locally as mud holes. Excavation of the first mud hole began in the late 1890s[1], and horses were used to haul trucks laden with clay from the pit[1]. Today the mud hole forms a lake, and the aggregate causeway upon which railway lines once lay remains partly above the water line. The causeway is composed of rounded flint, fused ash and refractory (kiln) bricks. The rounded nature of the causeway flints may indicate that the flints were the by-product of a slurry wash mill. At the eastern bank of the first mud hole stood horse stables[1&2], and what is widely regarded to be a brick horse trough of the Victorian/Edwardian era remains at the site to this day.

The aggregate causeway into the first mud hole, now flooded.
Here, horses were once used to haul trucks loaded with clay from the pit.
Photograph by Clive Tester 2006.

Views due east and due west across the aggregate causeway into the first mud hole.
Photographs by Clive Tester 2006

On the aggregate causeway: left photo shows a section of railway line and the right photo shows an iron peg (rail spike) used to secure railway lines to sleepers. Many rail spikes like these lay among the flints of the aggregate causeway into the first mud hole. Note the rounded nature of the flints that may indicate their origin as a slurry wash mill by-product. Photographs by Clive Tester 2006.

The lake that formed in the first mud hole. It is interesting to speculate as to why this mud hole was excavated in such a way that a section of land was left undisturbed in the centre of the pit. In later years the pit became flooded with ground water and this isolated piece of land became an island. Could it be that those who were responsible for the pit's formation did this in foresight of a time when the pit would be disused and become a lake? Perhaps those Victorian/Edwardian muddies and civil engineers were looking to the future aesthetics of the lake that would eventually form. Their legacy certainly lived on. Seventy years hence, I would oftentimes swim to this island. There I would find a copse of long grasses and hawthorn trees that knew only of the touch of the wind. In the mind's eye of my boyhood it represented a unique little world long isolated from the surrounding land: a microclimate in its own right with its own unique ecology. Today, swimmers no longer visit this little island. For at the dawn of the 21st century the lakes of Cliffe Marshes became part of a nature reserve managed for the provision of a safe haven for bird life. Perhaps this little island is symbolic of our marshes in its splendid isolation along the banks of the Thames estuary. Long shall it remain. Photograph by Clive Tester 2006.

The old perimeter fence around the first mud hole built from railway lines.
Photograph by Clive Tester 2006.

Brick structure located in the area of the stables of the first mud hole.
This structure is regarded locally to be a horse trough of the Victorian/Edwardian era.
Photograph by Adrian Hatcher 2015.

The Slater family of Cliffe Creek c.1910 with Mr (Tubby) and Mrs Slater. Front row: far left is Herbert, the girl second from the left is Mildred AKA Aunt Sis, the boy third from the left is George, the boy in front of Tubby is Albert. Back row: middle is Ellen and the girl on the right is Kate. Aunt Sis at the time when this photograph was taken was witnessing the industrial heyday of olden Cliffe. Photograph courtesy of Don and Ross Pople.

THE SECOND MUD HOLE

Near to the eastern most end of Creek Road the footpath diverged from Creek Road to cross a field. (With the clay extractions with pontoon cranes of later decades this field became what is known locally as the Pontoon lakes). The path continued onto a footbridge that crossed a narrow section of the second mud hole to be dug at this site.

Old maps together with Aunt Sis' childhood memories indicate that excavation of the second mud hole began soon after the turn of the century. From the footbridge the path continued toward the direction of Black Path. Aunt Sis recalled her memories of the year 1909 when muddies could be seen digging clay in the second mud hole almost immediately below the bridge on which she and her school friends walked. The muddies' job employed a skilful technique. Using a long-bladed spade, a slab of mud was chopped from the mud face in seconds with the last cut inducing the slab to fall onto the spade. The slab was then tossed in the direction of a waiting railway truck then immediately the next slab was cut and almost on the spade before the previous slab had landed in the railway tuck. The 2-foot gauge railway system of the second mud hole operated on a mechanical pulley system. The trucks were pulled from the clay pit to the cement works by means of a long steel cable wound to a large rotating winch at the factory in the Francis Chalk Quarry[1].

In the second mud hole stood a wind pump; it was a pump of the Dando Company. The wind pump became known locally as the Dando. Its purpose was to keep the mud hole from flooding with ground water that would have continually seeped into the clay pit from the surrounding marshland.

The wide-angle perspective of the drawing on the following page incorporates widely spaced elements of the second mud hole and the Francis Chalk Quarry beyond. The drawing represents elements that were operational over the period of the first two decades of the 20th century. Muddies are shown digging clay from the pit which had a depth something in the order of 20 feet below the level of the marshland. In the background, the hill upon which Black Path ascends had fewer trees than today. Near to the foot of Black Path stood an iron chimney[1], and it was most likely supported by steel cables. The chimney served a stationary steam engine the purpose of which was to pump water from the chalk quarry[1]. It was one of three sources of water for the Francis cement works. At the perimeter of the chalk cliffs are depicted a row of bottle kilns. The water sources and the bottle kilns are discussed in detail in the Francis Chalk Quarry section.

The footbridge over the second mud hole in the early 20th century.
This wide-angle perspective aims to capture widely dispersed elements within the area and is not intended to be a scale accurate depiction. Copyright Richard Bizley 2014.

The geographical context of the drawing on the previous page can be viewed in the map at the end of this chapter. The scene depicted in the drawing was reconstructed from the memories of Aunt Sis along with modern day photographs.

The footbridge over the second mud hole. Photograph by Clive Tester 2006.

The same viewpoint eighty years earlier in the 1920s. The people in the photograph are from the Green family who lived at Green Lane Cliffe in this period. Photograph courtesy of Vivienne and Kevin Duvall.

[The bank of the original mud hole]

The railway lines of the second mud hole that were in operation in the first two decades of the 20th century. The remaining marsh land around the original mud hole was later excavated by the use of pontoon cranes in the 1950s and 1960s. Photograph by Clive Tester 2006.

[The remains of the Dando]

[Remains of the footbridge]

[Cable roller]

The railway lines of the second mud hole. Photograph by Clive Tester 2006.

Cable roller

The looking due west over the second mud hole. Photograph by Clive Tester 2006.

The railway lines of the second mud hole. Railway sleepers are still intact.
Photograph by Clive Tester 2005.

Left: A cable roller with its steel cable still present. The railway line of the second mud hole, photograph by Clive Tester 2006.

Below: Looking due northeast across the second mud hole. The pipe is what remains of the Dando wind pump. Photograph by Clive Tester 2006.

An iron barrel-like structure located at the western most bank of the second mud hole: This artefact was once part of the water management system of the second mud hole during the early 20th century[1]. Photograph by Clive Tester 2006.

THE FRANCIS CHALK QUARRY

The Francis Chamber Kiln with the testing house in the foreground. Likely taken just prior to the demolition of the chimney it shows the essential elements of the Francis Chalk Quarry during its industrial period. Photograph from an unknown local source.

The quarry was owned by I C Johnson and Co Ltd from 1874 and sold to Francis and Co Ltd in 1886[7]. Cement production at the quarry began in 1874[7]. Over a time spanning from 1874 to 1898 an assortment of kilns was constructed in this quarry[7]. The chamber kiln complex (arched faced structure) shown in the photograph on the previous page survives to this day and is referred to in this book as the Francis Chamber Kiln. While there is some uncertainty regarding the construction date of this kiln complex the maps at the end of this section indicate a time period: the kiln complex is absent in the 1872 map and appears by the time of the 1897 map. Two kilns were added to the northwest end of the kiln complex in or after 1897, and a further block of chamber kilns were added to the northeast end of the kiln complex at around the same time[20]. Jim Preston's analysis[20] puts a probable date for the additional kilns of between 1897 and 1899. The Francis works was amalgamated into the APCM in 1900. However, in Aunt Sis' childhood and early adulthood, the factory was still known as the Francis works. And during this period, the APCM was referred to locally as the Combine.

The photograph on the previous page shows the Francis Chalk Quarry as it would have appeared sometime after its closure in 1921 when its industrial infrastructure was still largely intact. During Aunt Sis' childhood and early adulthood in the early 1900s, chalk for the cement works was dug by hand from the cliffs of the Francis Chalk Quarry by workmen suspended by the waist on ropes. The chalk was picked from the cliffs to fall directly into railway trucks stationed below.

A locomotive in the Francis Chalk Quarry. The driver was Sid Francis and the Points Boy was Herbert Slater (brother of Mildred, AKA Aunt Sis).

Photograph courtesy of Don and Ross Pople.

The drawing of the second mud hole that appears earlier in this chapter shows a series of bottle kilns before the cliffs at the northern end of the Francis Chalk Quarry. When commissioning the drawing, I based the bottle kilns on various local accounts of there once being a bottle kiln (or kilns) at the bottom of Black Path together with information from the 1908 ordnance survey map shown at the end of this chapter: the 1908 map shows a series of nine kilns in the northern part of the quarry. Dylan Moore[7] questions whether the structures marked as kilns in the northern part of the quarry on the 1908 map were indeed kilns. Dylan Moore's analysis of the area brings the possibility that the structures had been mistakenly labelled as kilns on the 1908 ordnance survey map, and that these structures may have been hoppers for rail loading of hand-milled chalk. Substantial remains of four structures located in the area marked as kilns on the 1908 map survive to this day. These remains may one day provide some answers to the question: were these structures kilns or were they chalk hoppers or did both types once exist at this location in the quarry?

Left: The remains of a structure located in the area marked as kilns on the 1908 map. It is located within the thicket that lays before the cliff in the photograph on the right. The foreground of the photograph on the right is in the location known today as the Apples (Refer to the map in chapter 4). Photographs by Clive Tester 1983.

The remains of a structure located in the area marked as kilns on the 1908 map.
This structure lays at the side of a hill that is known today as Cliff Face.
Left: Part of the arched entrance to the structure. Right: the structure interior.
Photographs by Clive Tester.

In May 1872, I C Johnson obtained a patent for what became known as the Johnson chamber kiln[8]. The design of the chamber kiln represented an advancement on the earlier bottle kiln. The chamber kiln was essentially a bottle kiln the hot exhaust gasses of which were ducted through a horizontal slurry drying chamber. This amalgamated the processes of slurry drying and slurry firing into a single kiln complex. It represented an improvement over the earlier bottle kiln technology in the efficiency of the process both in terms of ergonomics and the use of fuel. The chamber kiln complex shown in the image on page 20 was composed of a series of kilns. The kilns resided at both ends of the structure. The hot gas from the kilns was ducted along horizontal channels (the furrowed structure at the top of the complex) to dry the cement slurry of the next batch. The photograph shows raised panels on the roof of the drying chambers. These were removed for various operations that had to occur between firings of the kilns[1]. A J Francis[8] referrers to inlets at the top of the drying chamber into which slurry was pumped until the slurry layer in the drying chamber reached 8 inches in depth.

Coke for the Francis Chamber Kiln pictured on page 20 was brought via a railway that ran along this flint embankment bordering the kiln. During the late 1970s George Slater, whose job in the earlier part of the century as a *coke boy* had been to load the chamber kiln with coke, showed me around the chamber kiln and this associated railway embankment as told on page 134.

Photograph by Clive Tester.

At the end of each heating cycle the kiln was left to cool. Workmen entered the drying chambers wearing wooden clogs[1] and dug out the dried slurry with a special pick like tool[1]. The dried slurry was fed into the kilns to make the next batch of cement[8].

Aunt Sis recalled to me how the kilns were loaded for firing: a layer of faggots was placed upon the iron bars at the very bottom of the kiln. Upon the faggot layer was placed alternate layers of coke and dried cement slurry. Lighting the faggot layer started the firing, and the kiln charge was allowed to burn through to completion. At the end of the firing the kiln was allowed to cool before workmen entered the kiln to dig out the cement clinker.

Bottle kilns were the first type of kiln to be used in cement production. They were a development of earlier beehive type kilns that were used to burn the forerunner of modern cement: lime.

The flat roofed building before the chamber kiln was known as the Testing House[1]. It was a material testing laboratory where quality control testing of the cement was performed. A good insight into the kind of testing that was performed by cement testing laboratories like these can be found in A. J Francis book: The cement Industry 1796-1914: A History[8]. The quality tests listed 1 to 4 below are defined in A J Francis book. Major A.J Francis is the great grandson of one of the earliest cement makers in Britain.

By the early 1900s, practices in the quality control testing of cement had matured from its start in Victorian times. The testing house was the remit of the cement chemist, and it is likely that the testing house at the Francis Chalk Quarry at Cliffe would have engaged in the following tests to assure the quality of the cement produced at the Cliffe site:

1. Compression and tensile strength tests: A sample of cement was cast into briquettes of a standard size. The briquettes were left to set for a standard period of time and then placed into a machine which recorded their breaking point when subjected to tension or compression forces: forces which amounted to several tons. An interesting note is that engineer Vitale de Michele invented such a testing machine at the Cliffe Creek cement works in the 1860s[8].

2. Specific gravity test: A measure of the weight per unit volume of cement was used as an indication of the degree of calcination (burning) of the cement and also its fineness[8].

3. Setting time: This was determined by use of a Vicat needle. A needle with a flat point of 1/10 inch and loaded with a weight of 3 lb was placed against a sample of cement that was in the process of setting. The needle was applied for 1minute intervals every 10 minutes. The setting time was defined as the time when the needle left no appreciable mark on the cement sample[8].

4. Fineness of grinding: The particle size of the cement was determined by passing a sample of cement through a sieve of a standard mesh size and weighing the residue that was retained on the sieve[8].

5. Salinity test: Estuarine clays like those found at Cliffe had a salt content that was potentially detrimental to the cement quality. Salinity levels in the raw materials were assessed[1].

An access point was built into the construction of the bottle and chamber kilns where the man responsible for the firing of the kiln, known as kiln burner, would take an in-process check sample. The sample was analysed to ascertain whether the cement charge had reached, in the burning process, the required quality[14].

Water was required for the operation of the cement works for the production of cement slurry which was a suspension of pulverised chalk and clay. Water would also have been required for the steam engines of the railway system which operated in and around the cement works. Three water sources existed on the site. As depicted in the map drawing at the end of this chapter a stationary steam engine operated in the deepest part of the Francis Chalk Quarry near to the foot of Black Path[1]. To this day, the iron chimney remains at the site, lying horizontally in undergrowth [1 & 22]. The chimney is constructed of riveted iron and is lined with firebrick. In modern times, the deepest part of the quarry is flooded for all but the driest of summers. This is testament to the function of that steam engine in keeping the quarry dry during its industrial period. The water seeps into the quarry from the surround chalk bed; as Aunt Sis used to tell me of the flooding of parts of the quarry in its post-industrial time: "water always finds its own level". A second water source lays beside Black Lane a few hundred feet to the west of the stationary steam engine site. The well is still in evidence to this day and is covered with a large concrete slab.

A third water source was located at the southern half of the quarry; in this area existed further sets of kilns. This part of the site was cleared around 1964 to make way for a petrol storage depot. The well is still in existence at the site of the former petrol storage depot[1]. Water for the Francis Chalk Quarry works was stored in a large water tank that was situated on the top of the chalk hill located on the northwesterly border of the chalk quarry[1]. The concrete plinth upon which the water tank sat is still in evidence at the top of the hill[22]. The chalk hill was also the location of two caves set into its southern cliff[1]. One of the caves housed a blacksmith's workshop[1]: this would have provided a metal working service for the engineering requirements of the site. During the clearance of the site for the petrol storage depot, the cliff face was extensively cut away leaving the caves truncated[1]. Soot from the blacksmith's fire is still in evidence on what remains on one cave wall [1&22]. The site would have also had mills for grinding the cement clinker into a fine powder. Somewhere within the Francis Chalk Quarry there existed a cooper's workshop[1]: in the early 20th century cement was shipped in wooden barrels[1].

SLURRY PRODUCTION IN THE FRANCIS CHALK QUARRY

A J Francis book[8] describes the evolution of the manufacture of cement in the 19th century and the advancements in the way in which cement slurry was processed. While A J Francis book does not describe specific details of the slurry processing plants at the Francis Chalk Quarry at Cliffe, the technological aspects of the following section are drawn from A J Francis book. This provides an insight into how slurry would likely have been processed at the Cliffe site between the 19th and the early 20th century. A more detailed analysis of slurry production in the early cement industry can be found in A J Francis' book.

The first stage in cement production is to produce a fine and intimate mix of the raw materials chalk and clay in the proportions of three to one in about five times their weight in water. This is known as slurry.

Slurry was blended in a wash mill. In principle, the wash mill consisted of a large circular tank. In the centre of the tank was a pier to which a horizontal beam was attached and from which blades were suspended. The beam was made to rotate thus affecting the break up of the chalk and clay and their complete mixing.

Slurry that was used for the earlier bottle kilns was pre-treated as follows: the slurry from the wash mill was allowed to flow into a large reservoir know as a back. The slurry remained in the back for several weeks to allow the solid material in the slurry to separate from the water. The top layer of water was drained periodically. The settled material was dug from the back and transferred to drying flats: these were covered areas of iron plating or fire-clay tiles heated from below onto which the slurry material was spread. Coke was required for the kilns, and it was produced in ovens the waste heat from which was conveyed through flues to the drying flats.

The chamber kiln allowed for this lengthy pre-treatment of the slurry to be by-passed. In this method of production, slurry was pumped from the wash mill direct to the chamber kiln[8] whereupon the exhaust gases of the preceding charge of cement drove off water.

Artefacts of the Francis Chalk Quarry that survived well into the 20th century reflect this evolution of technology as located in the image on the following page.

Quarry Cottages near to the Francis Chalk Quarry.

Photograph courtesy of Don and Ross Pople.

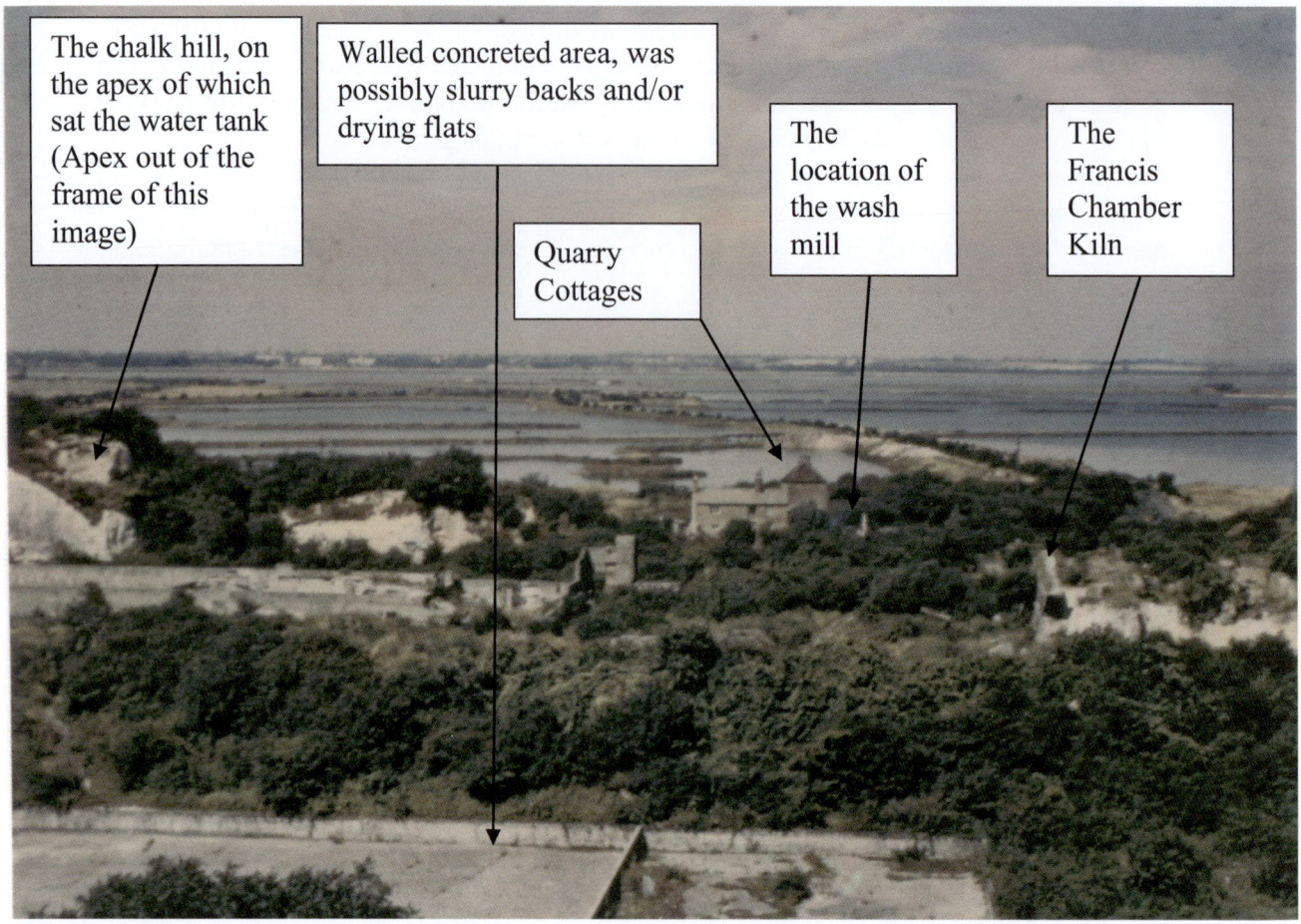

[Annotations on photograph:]
- The chalk hill, on the apex of which sat the water tank (Apex out of the frame of this image)
- Walled concreted area, was possibly slurry backs and/or drying flats
- Quarry Cottages
- The location of the wash mill
- The Francis Chamber Kiln

The Francis Chalk Quarry in the 1950s or early 1960s. Photograph by Albert Smith courtesy of Martyn Smith.

The large walled concreted area shown in the photograph certainly fits the description of a slurry settling back and/or a drying flat. In the period in which this photograph was taken, local people used the concreted area as a tennis court. Following the clearance of the site in the early 1960s for the petrol storage depot all but a few remnants of the walled concreted area remained.

During my childhood in the 1970s, the wash mill that was located near to Quarry Cottages was very much in evidence. The wash mill was situated on the opposite side of Black Lane and only around 10 metres from the front gate of Quarry Cottages. What remained of the structure during the 1970s was a large brick lined pit that was below ground level. At the centre of the pit stood a brick column. Protruding from the top of the column was a large screw threaded iron bolt. The column would have supported the rotating structure used to mix the slurry. Running down the western wall of the wash mill pit was an iron pipe; its location may have indicated its purpose: the wash mill stood adjacent to the chalk hill with its water tank to the west. It is possible that the iron pipe was for feed water drawn from the tank on the hill. Further evidence still in existence at the site to this day may support this postulate: in the undergrowth exists a ceramic pipe running down the chalk hill from the location of the water tank to the direction of the wash mill.

After over 100 years and still looking as good as new, the ceramic pipe on the chalk hill near to the location of the wash mill. Just a few feet from the pipe is the structure in the top right image. Its purpose so far remains a mystery. Photographs by Adrian Hatcher 2015.

It was to this wash mill that the cable railway line from the second clay pit likely ran. And by a mechanical mechanism, the clay-laden trucks tipped and deposited their load of clay as they passed the pit. Trucks laden with chalk would have come to the wash mill via the railway lines that ran from the chalk cliff face of the Francis Chalk Quarry. Associated with the wash mill would have been a weighbridge to proportion the chalk and clay. The finished slurry was pumped to the Francis chamber kiln that stands around 20 metres to the east[1].

The wash mill was completely filled in along with other changes to the area that occurred during the building of the sea wall defences in 1981: see chapter 4. A word of caution to any future industrial archaeologists who may wish to excavate the wash mill in centuries to come: up until its complete burial, the pit of the wash mill had become a dump of all manner of domestic and industrial waste materials.

Picture drawn from my memory of what remained of the wash mill in the Francis quarry in the 1970s. The figure of an average sized man gives an idea of the scale of this structure.

This circular area of bramble bushes grows over the area where the wash mill now lies buried. The bush covers an area approximately equal to the area that the wash mill covered. To the west stands the chalk hill where the water tank once stood. To the right is Black Lane. A century before, the wash mill and its associated machinery stood here and around it ran the industrial railway lines that brought chalk and clay to the wash mill. Within the undergrowth to this day can be found sections of steel cable left over from the cable-drawn railway that brought clay from the second mud hole. Photograph by Clive Tester February 2016.

A little less than a mile to the west of the Francis Chalk Quarry a factory of the new era of cement production was taking shape in the second decade of the 20th century. This factory would use the new rotary kiln technology: a process that would revolutionise cement production. Under the ownership of the Thames Portland Cement Company, construction of the "New Factory" as it was known to Aunt Sis and her generation started in 1910[1]. The factory opened for production in 1913[1].

THE EVOLUTION OF THE FRANCIS CHALK QUARRY AND ITS ASSOCIATED CLAY PITS.

Prior to the arrival of the cement industry at Cliffe in the early 1850s, chalk was excavated from the area that later became known as the Francis Chalk Quarry. Chalk from the quarry was used as a source of lime rock[7]. In this earliest period of operation, chalk was conveyed from the quarry to Cliffe Creek via a canal that was built at the end of the 18th century[7]. Jim Preston's section *Industrial Landscapes* in the RSPB commissioned report[21] draws on documentation of the time. It shows that by 1791, what were described as "lime works" at the "chalk cliffs" and a canal to the northwest "lately cut" were present at the site. The report[21] refers to a document dated 1818 that shows that by that time there was no lime works (kilns) at Cliffe. The 1818 document spoke of chalk being taken by horse drawn punt on the canal to the creek to be used for a variety of purposes: to make whiting, to be loaded onto barges for use in agriculture, to be taken to lime works elsewhere or to be taken as large blocks for making sea walls. A whiting factory was constructed before 1842 and is referred to as Chalk House on the Tithe Map[21]. It is worth noting as mentioned earlier in this chapter that Chalk House was still a feature of the creek in the early 1900s as recalled by Aunt Sis. The canal as a means of chalk conveyance continued with the advent of the cement industry at Cliffe Creek in 1853 and, as previously mentioned, was later superseded by a railway system in the early 1870s.

The land holds memories for future generations. Left photo: John Mark Tester looks into the dry remains of the 18th Century canal at Creek Road. Middle: the overgrown canal bed. Right: a rail spike of the 19th century railway system on the path to the Crystal. Photographs by Clive Tester May 2021.

A source of clay was required for the cement works at Cliffe as it grew and evolved from the early 1850s into the 20th century. The earliest definitive account of clay being excavated from inland (non-tidal) areas of Cliffe marshes was with the first mud hole referred to earlier in this chapter: this dates from the late 1890s[1]. The salt marshes along the rivers Thames and Medway provided a source of clay[19]. Indeed, I C Johnson's 1853 21-year lease at Cliffe Creek allowed for clay digging outside the sea wall and in Cliffe Creek[21]. However, the modest output in the earliest period of cement production at Cliffe required relatively little clay: around 50 tons per week[7]. Clay digging from the saltings close to Cliffe continued into the 20th century: during the early 1900s, clay was still being dug by hand from Cliffe and Higham creeks as recalled by Aunt Sis from her childhood. At the publication of this book, no firm evidence was found for clay excavation from an inland source prior to the late 1890s. It is possible that the first mud hole of the late 1890s represented the first inland excavation of clay at Cliffe. The following sequence of maps shows the development of the Francis Chalk Quarry and mud holes through a period of rapid growth in the industry of this area:

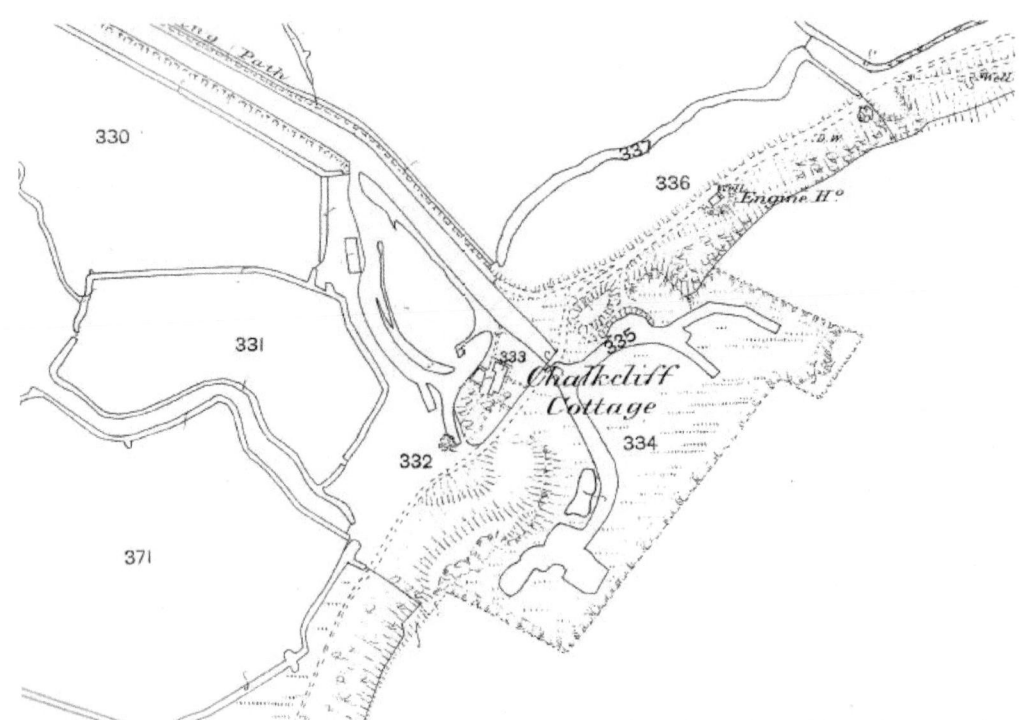

1872 Ordnance Survey map. Note the canal and associated towing path to the northwest to the direction of Cliffe Creek to where chalk from this quarry was destined.

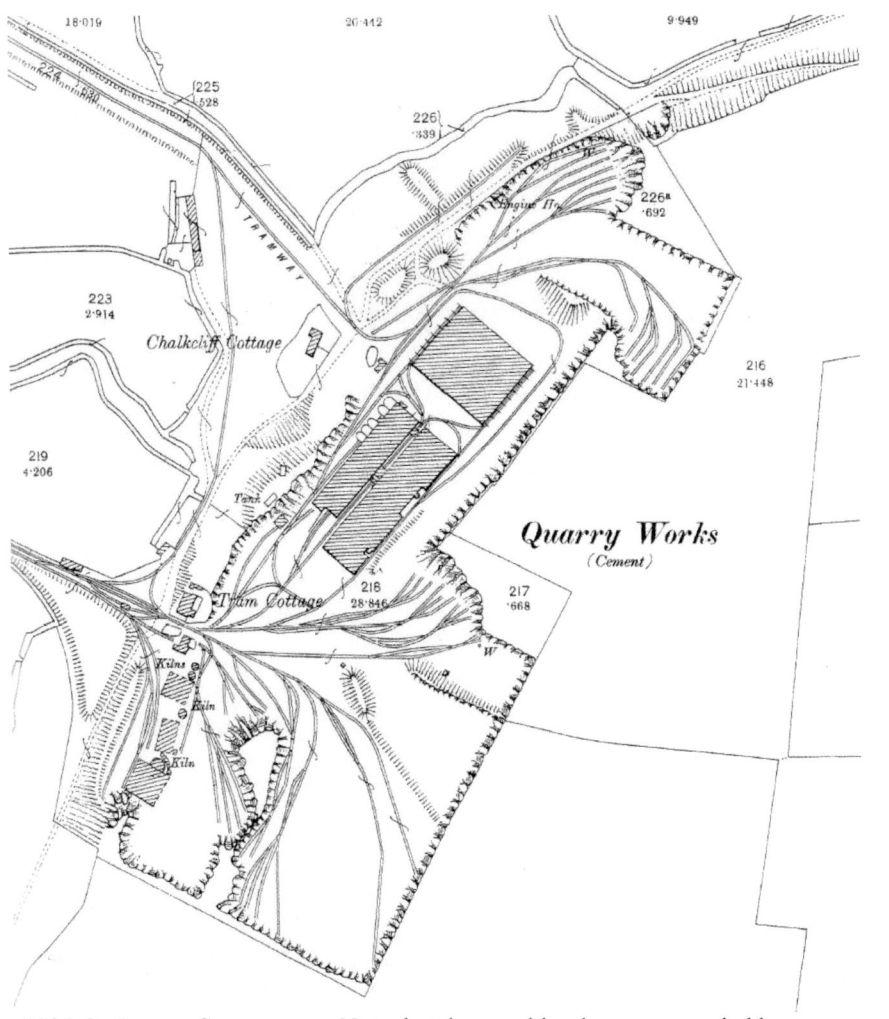

1897 Ordnance Survey map. Note that the canal has been superseded by a tramway, and note the industrialisation of the Francis Chalk Quarry.

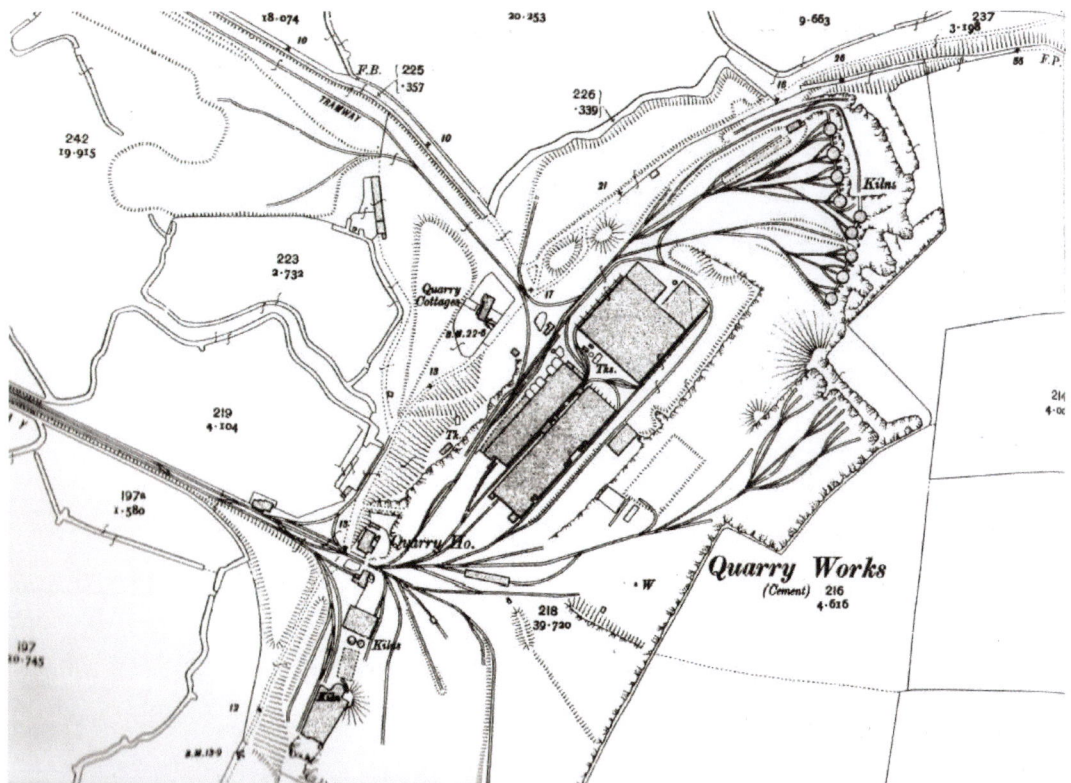

1908 Ordnance Survey map. Note the change in names from the 1897 map: Chalk Cliff Cottage has been renamed Quarry Cottages, and Tram Cottage has been renamed Quarry House. "Kilns" near to the northern cliffs, and an additional two banks of chamber kilns (centre), have appeared since the 1897 map was published.

The Francis Chalk Quarry in its industrial heyday. The Francis Chamber Kiln is centre, and apparent are the two smaller banks of chamber kilns which were added between 1897 and 1899 (structures nearest to the camera.) Immediately to the right of the tallest chimney is the water tank upon the chalk hill. Quarry Cottages are at the extreme right of the picture. Photograph courtesy of Dave Green, www.cliffehistory.co.uk.

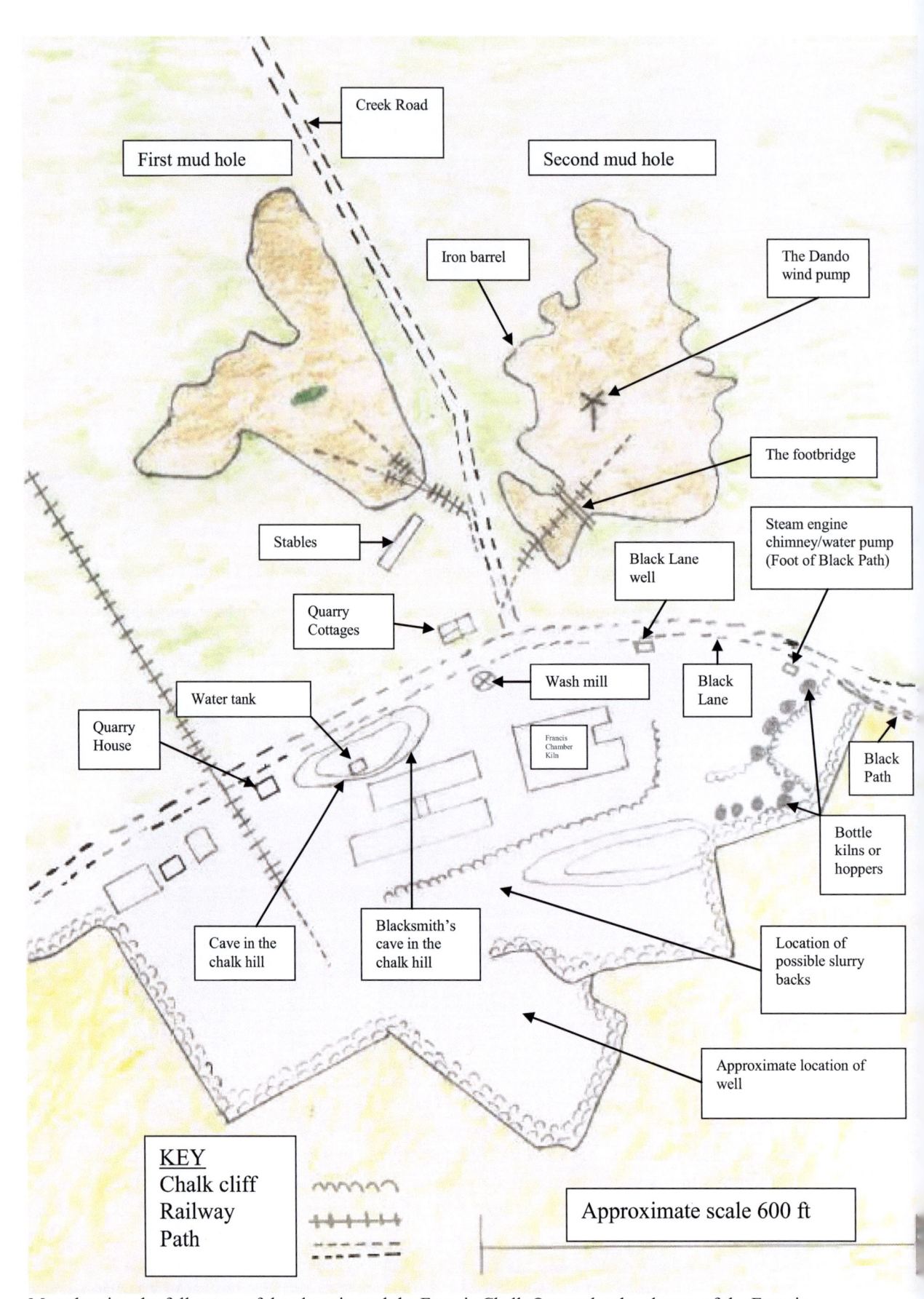

Map showing the full extent of the clay pits and the Francis Chalk Quarry by the closure of the Francis works in 1921. Not all of these features were in operation at the same time.

After our lengthy tour around the Francis Chalk Quarry, let us return to Aunt Sis' walk to school which would have taken them from the area of the Francis Chalk Quarry along either of two paths: Black Path or Black Lane. It is interesting to speculate from where the names of these paths derive. It could be postulated that the names derive from the cinders that formed the paths. The most likely source of the cinders was the cement kilns of the Francis Chalk Quarry. There are indeed areas of Black Path where cinders are still in evidence today, and in sections of the old route of Black Lane cinders can still be found (see chapter 4).

The next point of interest is Allen's Hill and its associated concrete bridge and iron railings. The bridge was constructed to facilitate the movement of vehicles on Allen's Hill that were destined for the Curtis's and Harvey munitions works a mile to the north[1]. The munitions works were operational between 1901 and 1921, and the Navy was the main customer of the factory[1]. Aunt Sis recalled that men and women walked from as far away as Higham for their daily work at Curtis's and Harvey. Tobacco and matches were prohibited from the site. Hence the Higham workers used to stuff all of their tobacco and matches into the hollow iron railings at Allen's Hill for retrieval on their walk home at the day's end[1]. And explosions were a great risk at the munitions works. Aunt Sis was witness to one such tragedy. One day while sitting in class at Cliffe School the sound of a mighty explosion rang out from the direction of the munitions works. Instinctively all at the school ran out to see what had happened: Aunt Sis and her class saw a high column of debris descending back onto works.

Via Philip MacDougall came five newspaper articles describing such accidents at the Curtis's and Harvey factory:

The Western Daily Press of the 19th February 1904 reported of a "disastrous explosion" with the loss of four lives and various injuries to other workers. According to the article, the explosion occurred at ten minutes before nine in the morning of the 18th February at the round house on the hill at the centre of the works. A column of debris shot high into the air which fell on to neighbouring buildings and causing damage. On hearing the explosion at Cliffe Village, the local doctor Dr Rogers immediately went to the works. Those killed were: William Know, Daniel O'Donnell, Jack Murray and William Talbot.

The Essex Newsman 4th April 1908 described a fire at the factory in which no one was injured. The fire was seen at intervals from Chelmsford.

The Grantham Journal, dated 18th June 1908 describes another tragedy: Julia Munn and Clara Goodyear were killed in an explosion in the dynamite department. Two others received injuries.

The Tamworth Herald 29 July 1911 describes several persons being killed and injured through an explosion at the site.

The Exeter Gazette of 22nd May 1914 describes an explosion involving nitroglycerine "that blew to fragments" one of the buildings at the site. The articles states: "The workpeople were warned by the fumes and hurried away in time".

Our thoughts must go out to those who were injured and to those who lost their lives in these tragedies and to the families of those people.

The year 1914 brought a tragedy of altogether greater scale: The Great War. Via Celia Cousins and Andy and Janet Keats a Chatham News newspaper cutting from 15 August 1914 reports on the effect of the war on the cement and the explosives works at Cliffe:

"The A.P.C.M., have notified their employees that any called to the colours shall so far as possible be reinstated in their positions on their discharge, and during the continuance of the war and their service with the colours the Company will make up the pay and allowance received by men and their wives from the Government etc., to their average weekly pay". The newspaper cutting continues: "Owing to the difficulty in obtaining fuel, both the A.P.C.M. and Thames Portland Cement Company, whose works have only recently started manufacturing, have had to go on short time, but Messrs Curtis and Harvey manufactures of explosives are working at full pressure, excepting that some of the female workers have had to stand off, so that there is comparatively little unemployment at present".

THE MUNITIONS WORKS: AN OVERVIEW

Two of the many old buildings of the Curtis's and Harvey munitions works.
Photographs by Clive Tester 1989.

English Heritage undertook a detailed archaeological survey and analysis of the Curtis's and Harvey explosives factory at Lower Hope Point between 2010 and 2011. The report[24] provides details of the history of the factory and its production. Hay, Merricks & Company Ltd established a gunpowder blending and storage facility at the site in 1892. The company was incorporated into Messrs Curtis's & Harvey Limited in 1898. From 1901 until its closure in 1921, under the ownership of Curtis's & Harvey, the factory was expanded to manufacture a range of explosives and propellants. These included gunpowder, gun cotton, nitroglycerine based explosives (cordite, blasting gelatine, dynamite, gelatine dynamite, gelignite) and Cheddites (chlorate-based explosives). The infrastructure of the factory extended over an area of around 128 hectares and included a range of reinforced concrete and brick structures some of which were covered by blast protection mounds. The site included tram beds and drains, buildings for drying gun cotton heated by hot air or steam, acetone recovery apparatus (acetone was used in the production of cordite), and acid handling facilities (mineral acids were used in the production of nitroglycerine and gun cotton). The site also included a mess-room, housing and jetties at the river.

One of the primary explosives manufactured on the site was gun cotton or cellulose nitrate. The product was manufactured in a wet state and required drying. In its dried state the material is prone to accidental ignition by friction or percussion. Another primary explosive manufactured on the site was nitroglycerine. By the accounts of inquest reports on which the English Heritage survey draws, nitroglycerine production was potentially hazardous and prone to accidental ignition of the high explosive product. The process involved the reaction of glycerine with a mixture of nitric and sulphuric acids, further processes to separate the nitroglycerine from the reacted mixture and purification by washing with water.

The site required large amounts of water. Water was sourced from a well located at Simmonds's Hole at Station Road Cliffe over a mile away to the south[11 & 28]. Water from the well at Station Road was channelled underground via a tunnel which led to a pump house which exits today at the southern end of Symonds Road[11]. The underground tunnel was wide enough to accommodate a narrow-gauge railway line[11]. When the tunnel was dug at the time when the munitions works was being built around the turn of the century, the railway line was used to convey small trucks used to take the chalk spoil from the tunnel face[11]. Given the copious amounts of water required at the munitions works, it is likely that water permeating out of the chalk tunnel itself provided water in addition to that from the well[11]. Via a 6-inch pump[11] at the pump house, the water was pumped through an underground iron pipe to the works at Lower Hope Point[11 & 28]. The iron water pipe traverses several ditches on Cliffe Marshes, and sections of the pipe that traverse the ditches are still visible to this day[28]. During the early 1970s, the well at Simmonds's Hole was excavated for use in farm irrigation, and some artefacts from its earlier use by Curtis's and Harvey were uncovered [28 & 29]. This included a small trolley that appeared to have been designed to run on rails[29]. Station Road has another legacy of the Curtis's and Harvey days: the houses in "The Crescent" were built for Curtis's and Harvey management on land owned by the company[11]; one of the houses was named Cur Har[11 & 28].

The English Heritage report[24] shows that the exact processes employed to produce nitroglycerine at Cliffe are difficult to identify because they were subject to continual change. The industrial mass production of this touchy high explosive was still in its infancy in the early 20th century. The processes used to manufacture this explosive were therefore prone to change as better ways of production were developed: the site in its short life must have been a place of innovation. A variety of explosive blends were manufactured at the site. These were blended combinations of primary explosives and given brand names. One type was named Cliffite[24] and it was used as a coal-mining explosive[30]. Interestingly, within the Cliffe vernacular of the 20th and 21st centuries, the term Cliffite was and still is used to describe an indigenous Cliffe person. It is interesting to speculate whether this colloquial term originated from the explosive brand manufactured at the Curtis's and Harvey works at Cliffe in the early 20th century.

The Chatham, Rochester and Gillingham News reported on the inquests into two explosions that occurred in 1904[25] (via Dave Green of the Cliffe at Hoo Historical Society). The document shows that two separate incidents occurred in the month of February 1904. The first occurred on the 4th February. This involved an explosion in a gun cotton drying room that killed outright George Kenknight and inflicted burns to William Moon from which he later died. The second explosion occurred a fortnight later during nitroglycerine production killing Daniel O'Donnall, William Know, John Murray and Elijah Talbot.

The inquest report[25] provides some insight into the day to day working at the factory. Personnel working in the gun cotton drying room were described as working in bare feet. Likely this was a practice enforced in order to prevent friction of boots against the floor which may have caused ignition of the products. Operations within the drying room at the time of the explosion were being conducted at night which suggests that a shift system was in operation. The night workers were using electric lamps, a relatively new innovation of its day, likely used to prevent accidental ignition. The report mentions taking the lamp back to the dynamo: apparently for re charging. The temperature within the drying room was controlled by use of two thermometers and the temperatures were recorded in a logbook. One of the thermometers was located in a place from where it could be viewed from outside of the drying room through a window, perhaps another safety feature. The temperature of an adjacent cordite-drying hut was described as being 100 degrees Fahrenheit.

The inquest report[25] into the nitroglycerine explosion shows something of the scale of operations. The explosion was reported to have taken place within a structure referred to as a "Round House"; within this structure at the time of the explosion was 1000 pounds of raw and 1000 pounds of refined nitroglycerine. The report shows that within the Round House the nitrating house was included. Nitrating is the chemical reaction whereby glycerine is reacted with nitric and sulphuric acids to produce nitroglycerine. A man employed in nitroglycerine production was called a Hillman: the earth protection mound enclosing the Round House resembled a hill.

The inquest report[25] describes a village in morning. A united memorial service to a large congregation lead by Rev. H. B. Boyd was held at Cliffe Church on Sunday evening 21st February. The funeral of William Moon was held on the following Monday and the funerals of the other men killed on the Wednesday. The report continues: "The whole district was in morning. The whole of the shops closed by arrangement early in the day, and business was entirely suspended; the public houses closed their doors while the funeral was in progress. There was scarcely a house to be seen that had not its blinds closely drawn, and people came from near and far to witness the sad ceremony".

A Round House at the Curtis's and Harvey site. Photograph by Adrian Hatcher 2015

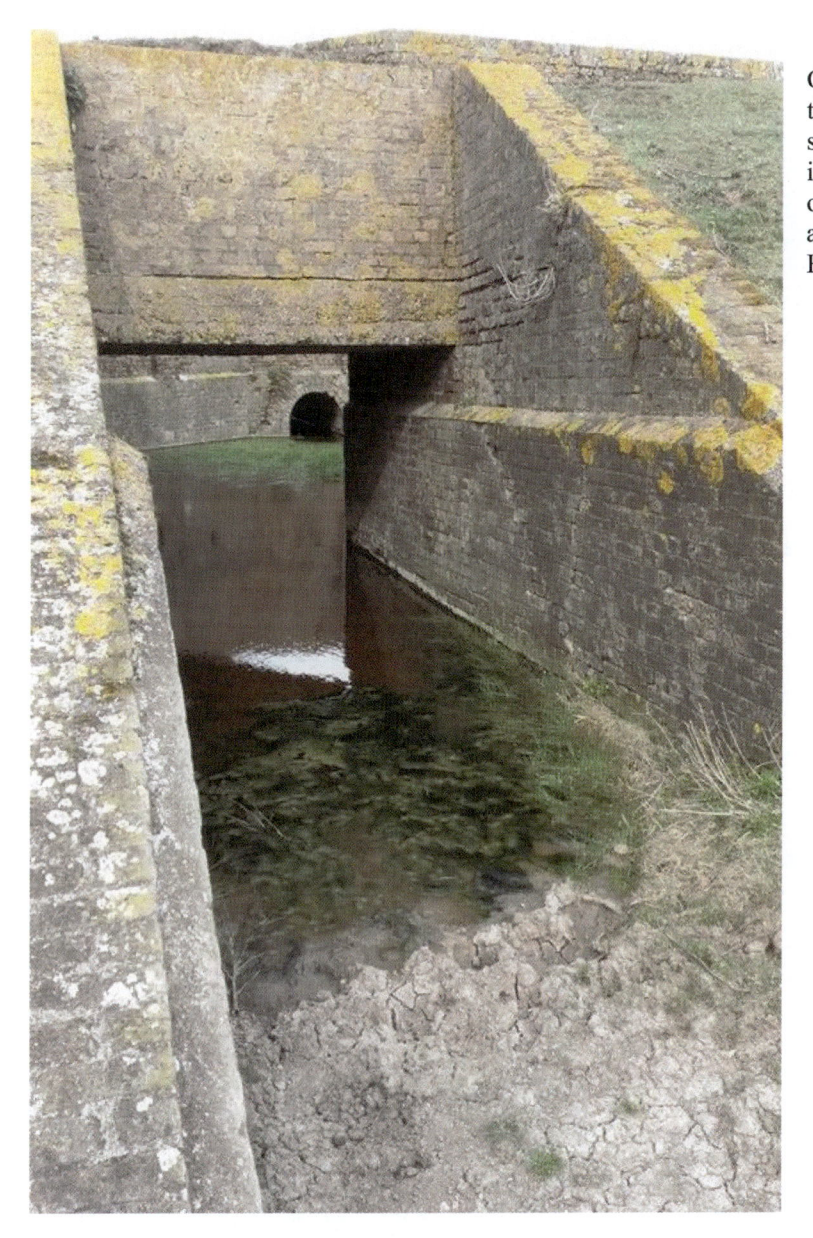

One of many large buildings that lay within the site. The size of this structure gives an indication of the scale of operations here a century ago. Photograph by Adrian Hatcher 2015.

A century hence, the Curtis's and Harvey site presents a picture of sublime isolation. The tides of the wide estuary ebb and eddy through its old wooden jetties just as they did back in its brief perilous dynamic heyday. Yet seldom today is the tide's daily progress through these relics witnessed by human eye. Those waterlogged wooden jetties are today the resting places of seabirds, and the Round Houses and long abandoned buildings that lay scattered across the marsh are now the sole remit of sheep and voles. By day birdsong fills the air and by night those empty shells of brick and reinforced concrete lay silent in darkness. A wide ditch borders the old explosives works and it widens into a small fleet to the south west of the site[28]. Within that fleet lays an island of reeds upon which rests a white stone: it is the watermark stone of the old Curtis's and Harvey works and it is marked with a water level line that was the highest permitted in the matrix of ditches linked throughout the Curtis's and Harvey site[28]. Back in the day, once this water level was exceeded, a manual sluice was opened from the fleet into the river[28]. The stone's instruction of water level is expressed in a few words that today still read clear. Those short words stand bold as if they still speak to those who once worked here: folk long gone; some of them most tragically before their time.

The watermark stone. Photograph by Clive Tester June 2015.

The watermark stone.
Photograph by Clive Tester June 2015.

Above: In its dynamic heyday munitions workers at Curtis's and Harvey circa 1914. Joy Daniels' mother is in the middle row third from the right. Photograph courtesy of Vivienne and Kevin Duvall.

Right: Stillness and silence a century hence. Photograph by Adrian Hatcher 2015.

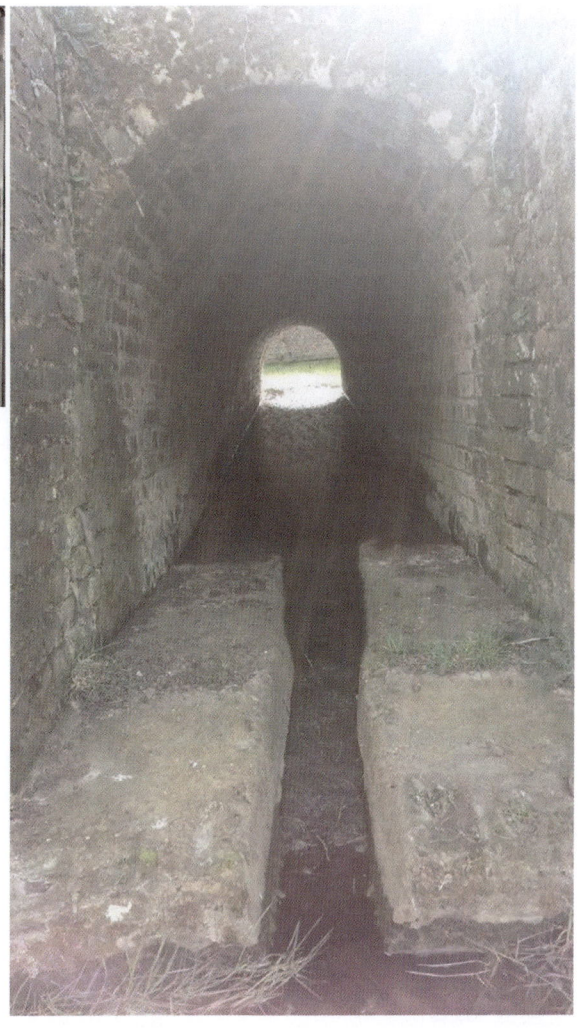

Curtis's and Harvey jetty. Photograph by Clive Tester June 2015.

CHAPTER 2

THE DAYS OF "THE MUD 'OLE"

THE 1920S 1930S AND 1940S.

The Burton family at No 6 Turner Street in the 1930s:
Back row: Uncle Eddie, my grandmother Alice and my grandfather Ernest, Aunt Sheila.
Mid row: Aunts Kate and Madge.
Front row: My mother Gwen and Uncle Sid.
The top of Uncle George's head is just in the frame of the photograph before Eddie.
At this time Uncle John and Aunt Rita were babies.
Photograph by Lilly Millgate nee Roberts.

The family Burton: Ernest Edgar b. 4th July 1880 and Alice Kate b. 1st May 1889 and children George b.1912, Edgar "Eddie" b.1914, Sid b.1916, Sheila b.1918, Madge b.1922, Kate b.1925, Gwen b. 1927, John b.1930 and Rita b.1932.

At No 6 Turner Street Cliffe in the early 1930s my mother and her siblings carried a candle up the stairs to bed at night. Nighttime, a candle was kept burning on a chest of drawers located at the top of the stairs. Later my grandmother bought a glass oil lamp for the landing. The girls, Sheila, Madge, Kate, Gwen and Rita slept in the big bedroom at the front of the house. The boys, George, Eddie, Sid and John occupied the mid room. My grandparents had the small box room at the back. The family had initially lived at No 19 Millcroft Road and had moved to No 6 Turner Street in the early 1930s because it had an extra bedroom. The Turner Street houses were originally built for workers of the Francis cement works and named Turner after a Francis works manager or chemist[11].

Rita and John Burton at No 19 Millcroft Road in the early 1930s.

Oil lamps lighted the downstairs rooms; the lamps were suspended from the ceiling on a cord to allow them to be lowered for filling. My mother recalls that the lamps also gave out heat. This was welcomed in winter months as the family could afford to keep only one fire in the house which was a Kitchener stove in the kitchen.

It is often said that it was by virtue of the cement works (then under Thames Portland Cement) that electricity came to the village in the 1930s. Electricity came to Cliffe when my mother was around 5 years of age which places the year around 1932. Among the residents of Turner Street there was much conversation and debate regarding the coming electricity. Some were reluctant to make the change.

The toilet was shared with the neighbour and was located in a narrow brick shed on the garden boundary. The drainage from the toilets of the terrace of 32 houses fed into a communal cesspit that was located close to the house of William Pepper a few doors down from No 6 Turner Street. In his back garden was a hand pump that was used to remove wastewater from the Turner Street cesspit. It was Mr Pepper's job to operate this pump. This was performed once a week, and my mother recalls that it took Mr Pepper the best part of a working day to complete. Mum remembers William Pepper of the 1930s as a man of advancing years. In his younger days, William Pepper was a muddie working in the clay pits of olden Cliffe.

Post card showing William Pepper at work in a clay pit at the Cliffe cement works. The inscription on the back of this post card reads: William Pepper. Mud diggers at cement works.

Post card courtesy of Joy Daniels.

William and Roseana Pepper were Joy Daniels' maternal grandparents.

A tap in the garden of No 6 Turner Street, shared with the neighbour, was the source of water for the household. Three buckets of water were kept on the kitchen table. The buckets held water to fill a kettle and a bowl for washing. Each Saturday, a tin bath was brought into the living room. Through the evening each took turns for a bath. A little more hot water was added to the used water as each of eleven took their turn. At the end of the evening wastewater was carried to the garden.

A communal bathhouse was located at the southern end of Symonds Road which Sid frequented. The bathhouse was known as the Bothies and was built for single men who worked for Curtis's and Harvey. There was a cookhouse, dormitories, bathhouse and a clubroom with one snooker table. It became Cliffe Club when Curtis's and Harvey shut and the chairman was Mr Shacklady works manager of Curtis's and Harvey[11]. At 14, Sid started work at the Alpha. As a young man he bought a wireless radio with his wages. Sid had a fondness for the new music of the era: on a typical day in Turner Street in the early 1930s, as recalled by my mother, the sound of jazz music resounded through No 6.

Much of the food consumed at No 6 Turner Street was home grown. Granddad kept rabbits in the back garden of No 6; meat from the rabbits was prepared in the scullery of the house. Granddad grew an abundance of vegetables on his allotment situated to the west of the British Legion club at Church Street; Granddad also raised pigs on his allotment. When matured he sold the pigs at Rochester Market. Of the shops in Cliffe of that time was a sweet and grocery shop owned by Mrs Nuisance. The shop was located in an old cottage next to the Evening Star Pub. Mum and Kate would often say "We're going up Nuisance's". Granddad would always correct them: "No, it is Mrs Nuisance". My granddad was very proper, quietly spoken, straight-laced and respectful.

Mum recalls of her childhood in the 1930s the shops of Cliffe. Starting from Norwood Corner with Polly Ward's hardware shop situated on the opposite side of the alley from Tom Beslee's Sweet Shop. Polly Ward sold sweets and grocery too. At the site of what is today the surgery at Millcroft Road was a terrace in which stood Morrad's grocery, sweet and tobacco shop. Moving northward to the next row of houses at Church Street situated opposite the British Legion club. This row of cottages was the site from south to north of Weeks the butcher, a needlework and wool shop run by Mrs Edge and Mrs Green's shop that sold sweets, grocery and delicatessen. My mother remembers the meat cutting machine in Mrs Green's shop: Mrs Green would carefully cut cooked meat such as corned beef into thin slices. Mrs Green always had a look of intense concentration as she cut the meat; it was a delicate task. Lastly on the row was the baker's shop run by Mr Luckhurst. Mr Carrington took over that baker's shop around the start of the Second World War. My mother recalls that none of these shops sold fresh milk, only tinned milk. Fresh milk was delivered via the dairy. Back in the 1930s, milk was delivered on a horse and cart by Walter Edwards; my grandmother would often give the horse a carrot or sugar lump. Next to the Evening Star Pub was Mrs Nuisance' shop; then close by was a corrugated iron shed which housed a greengrocer. Next was the Co-Op shop which sold clothes and grocery. Whack Knight managed a meat counter associated with the Co-Op shop. On the western side of Church Street stood the fish and chip shop. Today a takeaway exists on that site. Close by on the same side of the road was the chemist shop run by Mr Channon. The Chemist also dealt with the development of photographs. Bentley's garage was to the south west of the Six Bells Pub opposite to which stood Swannal's farriery. Continuing along Church Street was Martin's newsagents which sold grocery toys and bicycles.

Further north along Church Street was Parker's grocery shop. Mr and Mrs Parker's son Jack flew transport aircraft in the Second World War. After the war, Jack left the air force to take over the management of the business. My grandmother paid into the Parker's Christmas club. Each Christmas she would receive for the family a big box of groceries that include oranges – not an every day item in the 1930s. Next to the Victoria Inn Pub was Horace Martin's bakery. Next to the bakery at Longford House was the post office. Opposite the post office stood the corrugated iron shed of 193 Church Street housing Bentley's bicycle repair shop. On the junction of Church Street/ Reed Street and opposite the Black Bull Pub was M A Brown's sweet shop. Around the year 1940, Mrs Brown died upon which her daughter who worked in London as a hat maker took over the management of the shop. The row of cottages at the junction of Reed Street/North Road housed a grocery store run by Mr and Mrs Johnson, Sturt the butcher's, a dress maker's shop run by Mrs Forrest and a sweet shop run by the Bett family. The Bett family also owned a small orchard on a patch of land opposite this row of shops at Reed Street. At the eastern end of Reed Street was Saunders' grocery shop.

My mother recalls of the 1930s that the baker Mr Luckhurst kept horses on the land opposite his shop; that land is now the village play park. Sometimes the horses escaped only to be soon recaptured. When these episodes happened, it was "the talk of the village".

Mr & Mrs Morrad's shop was where my granddad bought his pipe tobacco. My mother used to be given 6 pence to buy half an ounce of light shag that Mr Morrad kept in a brown jar. Mr Morrad would roll the half-ounce of tobacco up in newspaper. The tobacco cost 4 pence; the other 4 halfpennies granddad gave to his four youngest children. One time Mrs Morrad gave my mother and Kate a big tray of sugar nuts. Mrs Morrad said that these had been left in the shop window in the sun so they were given away free.

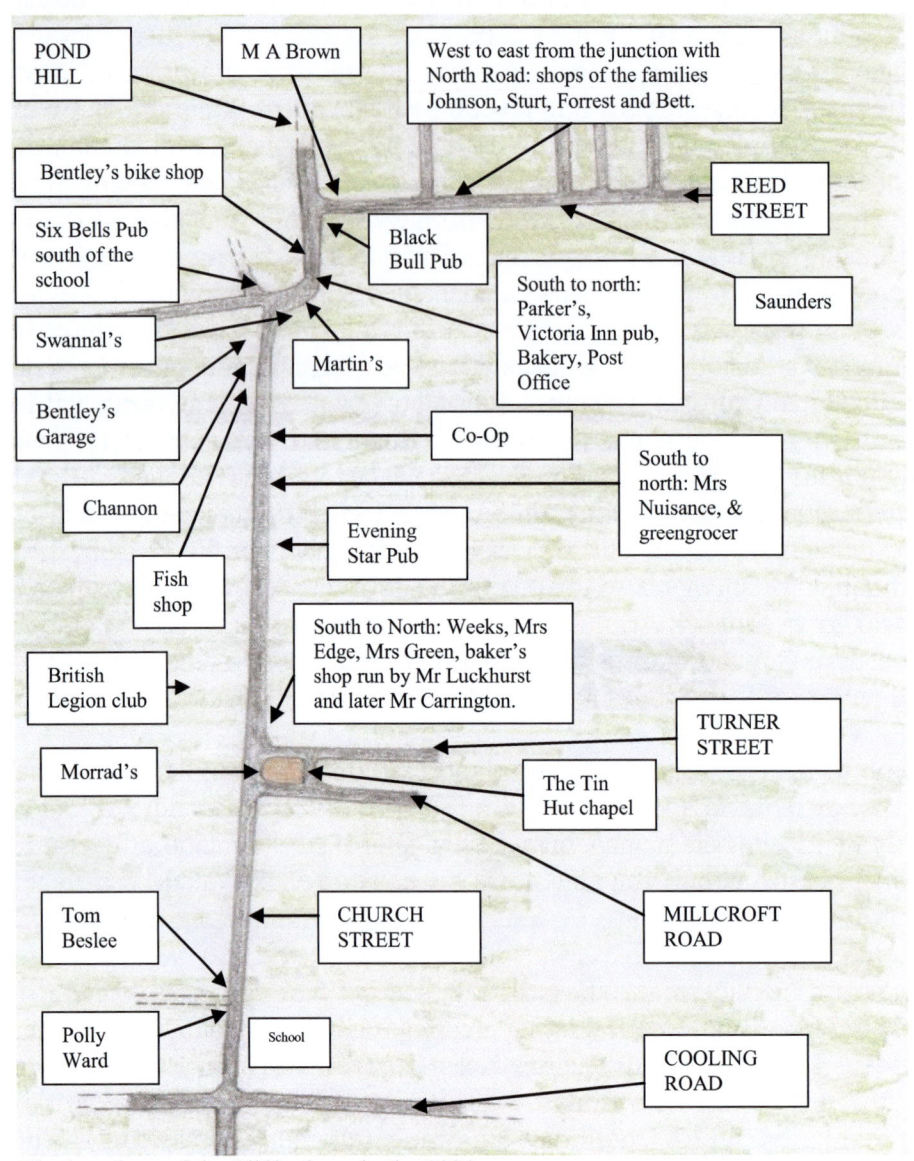

The locations of the Cliffe shops in the 1930s.
Drawing prepared from the memories of Gwen Tester and Evro Dockwray.

One source of entertainment in the village was the Globe cinema at Norwood Corner; this was one of the largest buildings acquired at the closure of the Curtis's and Harvey munitions works[14]. My granddad went to the Globe each week and always sat in the same seat near the front. My mother recalls that a Mr Whittaker owned the Globe, and the projectionist was Wally Seal. My mother recalls that the projector would sometimes break down, and folk would call out in jest "come on Wally, get it going". Wally would soon fix the projector and the film would resume. A ticket to the Globe cost 4 pence for a seat at the front. Courting couples could get a seat at the back for 1 shilling 9 pence.

During my mother's childhood in the 1930s, children went to the "tuppeny rush" at the Globe: This was Saturday morning cinema for children costing 2 pence. The children's Saturday morning cinema was mostly cowboys or Shirley Temple. During intermissions young ladies in smart attire would come around with trays of chocolate for sale.

My grandmother went to the cinema at Chatham every week. She would sit at the front row because her eyesight was poor. In fact, all she needed was a new prescription for her glasses, but she rarely spent on herself. The family kept a moneybox in the house containing coins collected for a rainy day. And my granddad often urged my grandmother to use the money in that box to buy a new pair of glasses – but she never would. Each week she would return from town on the bus and laden with heavy bags of shopping. Many of the bags contained apples for the family as Eddie and George loved apples.

Each year, the children of Cliffe were treated to the Co-Op carnival; this was organised by Mr Pierson of the Co-Op. A tea for the children was arranged on the recreation ground at the back of Mr Bentley's bungalow.

All children regularly attended Church in 1930s Cliffe. The children of the northern end of Cliffe tended to attend the churches closest in that location: Cliffe Church, the Wesleyan chapel on Church Street and The Plymouth Brethren chapel which was located about half-way along Reed Street. For the children of Turner Street, Millcroft Road and Norwood Corner, the "Tin Hut" as it was known was their local chapel. Cliffe Christian Mission worked from the "Tin Hut". Located at the western end of Turner Street it played a big part in the lives of the children. All of the Burton family attended the Turner Street chapel. My mother recalls that as children they attended the chapel twice on a Sunday and on Wednesday evenings too. Conducting the services were Mr Charlie Bachelor of New Barn Cooling and Mr Hagreen. A third preacher, an elderly man by the name of Mr Faulkener, rode his bicycle all the way from Swanscombe to attend the chapel. Mum and her friends attended chapel "in their Sunday best". At Easter, the girls wore their new Easter hat. The "Bartlett ladies" were the Sunday school teachers. The children looked up to these three sisters of the local Bartlett family.

Each year, the children were treated to prize giving at the chapel. The prizes were new books. My mother recalls a feeling of magic when entering the chapel on prize giving day to see all those new books neatly laid out. Prizes were awarded for learning and reciting a piece of text each week and for attendance too.

My mother recalls Harvest Festival at the Tin Hut and the fruit that the local farmers gave to the festival. In the era when fresh fruit was not available all year round, my mother recalls the fresh sweet smell of the fruit as they went into the chapel to buy the fruit for just a few coppers. Mr Carrington the baker donated small loaves; ingrained in the crust was a harvest pattern.

The ladies of the chapel organised the Christmas party, and in the summer the children went on a summer outing. The summer outing was held at Mr Batchelor's farm at New Barn Cooling. The children were taken to New Barn on horse and cart. In later years Ben Johnson's lorry was used: this was the same lorry that Ben Johnson used to take granddad's pigs to Rochester Market. Tea was held in the orchard where homemade swings had been assembled for the children. The farmer would come by with lots of apples and throw them into the orchard for the children to collect.

Inside the Tin Hut in the 1950s.
Picture courtesy of David Smith and Pastor James Ebbs.

The Tin Hut today.
Picture by Frila Tester January 2016

Back in my mother's childhood in the 1930s, the congregation of the Tin Hut sat on long pews to hear the sermon which was delivered from an ornate veranda. Music was provided via a large organ operated with a hand pump, and the congregation was kept warm in winter by a pot-belly stove which stood in the centre of the chapel. Later in the 1930s the large organ was replaced with a smaller foot pedal operated organ.

To this day, successive generations attend the Tin Hut chapel at Turner Street. Some of the young people who attended in the 1930s went on to have children who would likewise attend this chapel in later decades. My mother attended in the 1930s and her children Victor, Stella, Kay, Eric and Clifford likewise in the 1950s and 1960s. In 2014, my mother attended, at this same chapel, the dedication of her youngest grandchild John Mark Tester. The photograph on the left is of a Sunday school prize-giving event in the 1950s with Mr Wicker and Mr Hagreen. The boy in the shorts in the front row is David Smith. Today the Tin Hut has a thriving congregation.

Dave West of the Cliffe Community Church has provided the following information regarding the Tin Hut:

The land for the Tin Hut was purchased in October 1890 for £45, and the purchase of labour and materials for a 40 ft x 20 ft iron building was 100 guineas (£105) in January 1891.

From the late 1960s the local council started removing buildings in the area for re-development until the Tin Hut stood alone. With reduced numbers and a need for extensive maintenance costs the Trustees decided to close the building until further notice in August 1974. In November 1975 Jim and Beryl Ebbs (a local school teacher) supported by friends Dave and Rusty West had started a mid-week Bible Study meeting for local children at their home in Symonds Road. It became so popular that the numbers outgrew the space and Jim met the Mission Trustees who agreed to the Tin Hut being re-opened once again. After complete rewiring and new plumbing, the mid-week Bible Club transferred early in 1976 and the work there has steadily grown with new extensions added to both sides of the original building. More recently, Cliffe Christian Mission (a.k.a. the Tin Hut) was renamed Cliffe Community Church which, along with St Helen's, provides for the caring and spiritual needs of the community of Cliffe.

The Tin Hut following the Great Storm of October 1987. Note that part of the roof has been lost to the storm. A structure which was adjoined to the area around the blue door known as the "Stable" has been removed to allow for a new extension along the full length of the Mission: Photograph courtesy of Dave West 1987.

"GOING DOWN THE MUD 'OLE"

"We're going down the mud 'ole" was a phrase that my mother oftentimes heard from her teenage brothers. In the summer months, the teenage boys swam in the second mud hole: By this time the Francis clay pits had long been disused and had flooded with groundwater. Uncle Sid recalled to me in 2006 what he remembered about his boyhood escapades Under the Hill in the 1920s and 1930s:

My uncle George was known by an ironic nickname: Fatty. In fact, George was thin in stature just like his father. Eddie was known as Nutty. On the way to the mud hole, George Eddie and Sid Burton often stopped by at the Francis Chalk Quarry. Then, as was to be in my boyhood, this was a place of childhood adventure. There is a hill somewhat near the centre of the quarry composed of sandy clay that was known to George Eddie and Sid as Table Mountain. Just behind Table Mountain sat the disused chamber kiln. The boys would walk through an access tunnel that ran under the kiln complex to the base of the chimney. The tunnel was something in the order of 100 feet in length. Emerging from the tunnel and into the darkened cavern at the foundations of the chimney, the boys would peer up through that tall chimney to a small circle of light at the top.

The access tunnel under the Francis Chamber Kiln where once walked George, Eddie and Sid Burton in the 1920s and 1930s.
Up to the 1960s the tunnel was intact all the way through from the exterior of the kiln complex to the chimney foundations[6]. By the mid-1970s only around 40 feet of the tunnel was accessible. Photograph by Clive Tester 1983.

George, Eddie and Sid proceeded on to the second mud hole for a swim where the Dando wind pump was now the centrepiece of the lake that had formed in the old clay pit. The railway lines, which used to haul clay from the pit, now disused descended into deep water. The boys used to climb that wind pump to dive into the lake. That is until George during a dive encountered a hard object beneath the water that he later attributed to a submerged railway wagon. After that near fatal encounter the boys never again dived from the wind pump.

Top left: The chimney foundations of the Francis Chamber Kiln showing the access tunnel. Photograph by Clive Tester 1983.

Cliffe Marshes of the 1920s
Top right: Harold, Graham and Gordon Daniels play cricket near the Francis Chalk Quarry circa 1926. Photograph courtesy of Vivienne and Kevin Duvall.
Left: Cattle graze at the bottom of Allens Hill. Photograph circa 1926 courtesy of Vivienne and Kevin Duvall.

In the Picnic Grounds in the Francis Chalk Quarry the Green sisters and their children. Harold Daniels, father of Vivienne Duvall, is on the far left. Graham Daniels, future husband of Joy, is on the right. Joy Daniels provided the photograph of William Pepper on page 42. Photograph circa 1926 courtesy of Vivienne and Kevin Duvall.

George, Eddie and Sid Burton on the foot bridge over the second mud hole in the 1920s - 1930s.
Painting copyright Richard Bizley 2014.

Reunited in memories of "the mud 'ole": Eddie, Sid and John in the 1980s and George in the 1930s.

THE DEMOLITION OF THE FRANCIS CHAMBER KILN CHIMNEY

The Francis chamber kiln circa 1932. This photograph was given to the author by Aunt Sis.

Sid Burton recalled that the chimney was demolished one Sunday afternoon in the early 1930s; most likely in 1932. He along with many others sat at the top of the cliff that is shown in the background of this photo to witness the event. The village policeman Mr Clarke, who lived at Buttway Lane, was on duty at the demolition to prevent people entering the danger area.

A LOVELY DAY OUT

Ready for a picnic at the sea wall.
Kate and Gwen Burton at No 6 Turner Street, August 1937

While the boys generally spent leisure time at the mud hole, the girls spent summer days at the sea wall by Cliffe Fort. A lovely day out is how my mother described the sea wall by the Fort when she was a girl. The picture here was taken in 1937 outside No 6 Turner Street and the cases which Gwen and Kate are holding contained sandwiches and some of their mother's cakes. Gwen and Kate walked to the sea wall via Fort Road. On passing the Alpha, mum recalls the chimneys that were situated close to the road appeared to move when viewed from directly below: it was somewhat disconcerting. I would also experience this curious and somewhat vertiginous optical illusion decades later when I oftentimes passed the Alpha and gaze up to those towering chimneys. The sea wall at the Fort was known locally in the 1930s as the seaside of Cliffe. It was a place frequented by families on picnics; in the summer there were always lots of people there. Some folks paddled and some swam in the Thames.

A late summer pastime for my mother and her friends and family was blackberry picking at the Francis Chalk Quarry and at Creek Road. In its post-industrial period, the Francis Chalk Quarry had become known as the Picnic Grounds. The fires of the cement kilns of olden times had long since cooled, and weeds grew between the railway lines that once carried chalk-laden trucks from the cliffs. My mother and her school friends often climbed the steep paths of those cliffs: paths that had been trod by the chalk diggers of a previous generation. Mum's best friend was Ella Knight of Cooling Road. Some 40 years into the future I would climb the very same cliff paths with Ella and Reg Pennell's son Alec.

In those summer days Under the Hill, my mother, Ella and friends often called at Ivy House at the creek or at Quarry Cottages by the Francis Chalk Quarry for a glass of water. They were always welcome.

MEMORIES OF A CHILDHOOD WITH A SPECIAL FRIEND
BY GWEN TESTER

"Ella was my friend from the age of 5 when we both attended the infant school at Norwood Cliffe. Ella lived around the corner from the school; I lived in the middle of the village at Turner Street. I would call for her so that we could walk to school together. At the age of 7 we went to the "Big School" at the top of the village so Ella would call for me to walk to school together. I remember the Head Teacher at the infant school was Mrs Grist. The Head Teacher at the "Big School" at the Buttway was Mr Sibson. We were happy there especially at Christmas when the Vicar would give us presents from the Christmas tree. I remember hoping for the fairy from the top of the tree, but got Red Riding Hood instead, but loving that too.

Ella's grandmother Mrs Eliza Roberts was our neighbour when we lived at Millcroft Road. She was a good neighbour to my mum. I recall having a loose tooth or a cut finger or splinter, and my mum would say "Go to Mrs Roberts" and Mrs Roberts would always help. Mrs Roberts had sons the same age as my elder brothers, and Ella's mum was her daughter. I remember at that time firework night was shared with the neighbours: the families Jeal, White, Roberts and Cowling; it was an exciting time.

When the war came, Ella, I and other school friends were about 12. At the beginning, school was half of the day due to the war, but this changed to full days later on during the war. I remember when we all had to march around the playground practising carrying our gas masks. Once a week we school friends went to G.F.S: The Girls Friendly Society. On Sundays we attended Chapel at Cliffe Christian Mission in Turner Street.

We left school at 14. I went to work at the Doctor's house doing domestic work. Doctor and Mrs Rogers were lovely people to work for. Mrs Rogers learned to drive especially so that she could drive the Doctor around Cliffe and Cooling every day to do his calls and even in emergencies. Previous to that, he had made his house calls by pushbike. He also held surgery on mornings and evenings. Our doors were never locked in those days. I remember when Dr Rogers called at the house; if someone was ill, rather than knock at our door, he would whistle and then let himself in; so no need for a sick person to get to the door. Dr Rogers was a dedicated doctor.

Ella and I left the village for a couple of years to marry in the late 1940s. Returning to Cliffe we later became neighbours at Rookery Crescent with our children about the same age. Alec, Adrian and Clive were born in the same year with a few months between. I always remember the time when I had Clive in the pram, and Molly Hatcher came along Rookery Crescent with Adrian in his pram. Ella came over with baby Alec specially to see Adrian and Clive".

Gwen Tester nee Burton May 2015.

Ella Pennell nee Knight (1927 to 1967), and Reg Pennell (1918 to 1987) with son Paul at Rookery Crescent in 1953. Their family have a long association with Cliffe Marshes: Ella's family moved from Cooling Road to the Coastguard Cottages in the late 1940s. The Coastguard Cottages was the first family home of Ella and Reg Pennell before they moved to Rockery Crescent in July 1962. The Pennell family moved into 14 Rookery Crescent, which was the home of Ella's mother who duly moved into the newly built No 7 Wadland's Road[27]. Just as Ella and my mother spent summer days Under the Hill in the 1930s so did my siblings and I with Ella and Reg Pennell's children Alan AKA Mick, Paul, Penny and Alec. Photographs courtesy of Penelope Harris nee Pennell.

The family Roberts' strong association with Cliffe continued through the generations of the 20th and into the 21st centuries. Mrs Eliza Roberts' granddaughters, the children of Jack and Rose Roberts, Ann and Jean, married respectively Granville Bush and Ben Bishop. Their sons Robert, Graham and Alan Bush, and David, Mark, Paul and Martin Bishop along with Ella and Reg Pennell's family would share as children our strong affinity with Under the Hill as will be shown in chapter 4.

"COME ON TED, A KILN'S BROKEN DOWN AGAIN"

My grandfather Ernest Edgar Burton, known as Ted, at his allotment at Cliffe. The British Legion club stands in the background at the left. On the right, my mother can be seen looking over the fence with the corner of her hat just in the frame of the photograph. Photograph by Sheila Burton in the early 1930s.

In the 28 years that my grandfather worked at the Alpha, my mother recalls that oftentimes the foreman of the Alpha came calling on Alpha employees to help with some unexpected mechanical failure at the works at Salt Lane. This was commonly associated with one of the three rotary kilns that were at the core of cement production at the Alpha: their running was essential to meeting production deadlines. "Come on Ted, a kiln's broken down again" was the call at the door that my mother remembers of that time. Mr Butcher was a good foreman to his men; he looked after their interests[3]. These call outs often came in the middle of the night. But in the austere days of the 1930s this was always a welcomed call for overtime.

My grandfather came to Cliffe in 1910; firstly, lodging at No 12 Cooling Road. On Christmas day 1911 he married Alice Kate Wright of Hastings. In 1912 their first child George was born. My grandfather originated from Lenham Heath where he was partner in the Burton family butcher's business. He came to Cliffe to work at Weeks the butcher in the abattoir at the bottom of Turner Street. He was by training a butcher, and my mother recalls his highly professional approach to his trade. Later he worked at the Curtis's and Harvey munitions works at Lower Hope Point. Upon its closure in 1921 he went to work at the cement works at Salt Lane. During his employment at the munitions factory and later at the cement works he continued to provide a butcher's service to Cliffe. Aunt Sis recalled my grandfather visiting the Slater household at the creek to slaughter and prepare the chickens that her parents raised. Granddad's butchery trade was particularly busy around Christmas, and in his later years made for a lot of work.

The young Burton family c. 1920: George, Alice, Ernest, Sid, Sheila and Eddy.

Oftentimes, the talk at No 6 Turner Street was of the allotment and who was "murdering" the new potatoes by digging them up too early. My grandfather kept an immaculate allotment. My mother remembers that he would buy 6 runt piglets at Rochester Market, and raise them on his allotment behind the British Legion club. He would sell them on, once fully grown, back at Rochester market. My mother recalls a special time at the age of six or seven carrying a small bucket of pig feed following in the footsteps of her dad carrying his large bucket of pig feed. Often granddad would pull a large carrot from the soil of his allotment, take out his penknife, and carefully shave the surface mud from the carrot and give that fresh carrot to my mum to eat. Granddad would never peal a carrot or potato as this was considered wasteful. My mother recalls the fresh smell of the carrot after it had been slowly and patiently shaved perfectly clean by her dad. Granddad's celery was perfect: he would wrap newspapers around the base of the celery plants to prevent dirt from entering the stems. Mr Pierson grew gooseberries on the adjacent allotment. Mr Pierson would always give some of those big red gooseberries to my mother.

Paying of the annual allotment fee came each year at Michaelmas. This was something of a social occasion for which granddad wore his best suit and cap. It was a time for the men of the village to meet, and a chance to exchange anecdotes about the allotments. Payment was made at the Buttway Lane School. Headmaster Mr Sibson collected the annual fee, which was a nominal amount.

My mother remembers her father as a gentle modest mild-mannered man. He was a man of good humour too: sometimes if the topic of a far away country arose within a conversation he would joke "That's somewhere over Spendiff way isn't it?" Granddad lived to the age of 83. Even in old age, his allotment was kept immaculate and weed free. This was a quality helped more and more in his later years by Perce Springhall the husband of Sheila. At my grandfather's funeral, some 14 years after his retirement, Alpha cement managers Mr R. Osborn and Mr G. Butcher attended.

ALPHA CEMENT LIMITED

Long Service Certificate

CENTRAL
METROPOLITAN
OXFORD
RODMELL
THAMES

PRESENTED TO

ERNEST E. BURTON

in recognition of faithful Service rendered during the past 28 years and as a mark of appreciation and goodwill

Director

On his retirement from the Alpha in 1949 or 1950 my granddad was presented with this certificate.

Ernest and Alice Burton at the Alpha annual dinner at Symonds Road c.1940s or 1950s: The Alpha held an annual dinner for its retired workers at the Symonds Road club.

THE WAR YEARS

On leaving school, my uncle George worked for a garage located on the site of what is now 81 Church Street. The business was primarily fixing lorries. George joined the Marines at the age of 18, in 1930. He made the Army his career. George was based at Brompton barracks and also at Chatham Dockyard. He frequency came home on leave. Though he always left his departure on Sunday night to the last minute. George would only just catch the last bus out of Cliffe on a Sunday evening, much to the concern of my grandmother. My mother can picture George to this day, with no time left to tie his bootlaces, running along Turner Street with flailing laces to catch the last bus of the evening.

George sustained a foot injury after some years in the Marines, coming out of the Marines to spend 3 to 4 years back at home at Turner Street as an Army Reserve. George was born in 1912, which made him 15 years older than my mother. My mother remembers him more a fatherly figure than a brother, a role in which George happily engaged. He dressed as father Christmas for Christmas Eve; the suit he would have hired for the occasion. One Christmas, my mother recalls, he bought the girls each a doll of Dutch porcelain. In that time too, he married Dorothy Humphries. George was very much the family man. Each Christmas at No 6 Turner Street he made Christmas cakes, decorating them with grated coconut and sugar mice. He made pies, decorating the tops with leaves cut from pastry. In this time, he worked as a handy man about Cliffe: the money that he earned would be spent on the family. From the outbreak of the Second World War, George served in the Royal Army Ordnance Corps. George was killed at the battle of Arras aged 28 years on 20th May 1940.

Newly-wed George and Dorothy Burton
in the 1930s.

Uncle Eddie went to work at the Uralite in Higham on leaving school at 14. At around the age of 18 in 1932 he was laid off. Thus, Eddie went into the Army at 18 out of necessity as there was no work available locally. In the early part of the Second World War, Eddie was sent to France and was evacuated from Dunkirk in 1940. He didn't speak much about his experience at Dunkirk but did once give a hint to my mother of what the conditions were like: one badly wounded man on the evacuation boat sitting next to him died before they reached England. After Dunkirk, Eddie was sent to fight in Burma for the duration of the war. He made a career of the Army after the war, making Battery Sergeant Major. On retiring from the Army, Eddie worked as a postman. I remember Eddie on his frequent visits to Cliffe in the 1970s and 1980s. Quietly spoken, he was very much a gentleman, and a really good sincere man with a positive outlook about people. I imagine that he was very much like my grandfather. On his last visit to Cliffe, shortly before he died in 1992, Eddie made a special point of walking Under the Hill to visit the Francis Chalk Quarry and the Francis mud holes where he had spent many a halcyon boyhood day. Uncle Sid went to find him that day, and they returned together as they had done after many a day's swimming before the war.

Uncle Sid was based in England for most of the Second World War. Toward the end of the war he was sent to Italy. In Italy he had the opportunity to visit the grave of Aunt Madge's husband Ron Brown; uncle Ron had been killed while fighting in Italy. After the war Aunt Madge married Robert Thomas Springhall who was born at Buckhole Farm High Halstow in 1910. Uncle Bob worked at Chatham Dockyard during the war. In spite of illness he continued working as a labourer and sadly passed away in 1959.

The Second World War took Aunt Kate's fiancé Jim Ayers who died in action. In 1951 Kate married William George Hodd, known to us as uncle George, who had come to Cliffe to live at 16 Millcroft Road and was formerly from the Isle of Wight. He was a friendly, modest and an affable man of good humour. While he never spoke about his time in the army we believe that he was a Sergeant in the West Kent Regiment and his possessions show an Italian Cross as well as a photo of him that bears a Tel Aviv stamp.

Aunt Sheila's husband Perce joined the Scottish Fusiliers regiment in the Second World War. Uncle Perce was wounded when a shell exploded near to him during a battle in Madagascar. He lay wounded on the battlefield for several days before he was rescued and sent to a hospital in South Africa. Later he often reflected on how well he was treated by the staff at that hospital: they always brought the patients lots of fruit. A piece of shrapnel remained in his body until the 1970s when it was removed by the local GP.

Uncle John did his National Service in the late 1940s. In 1971 John married a lovely lady from London: Ruth Gwendolen Hayward. A genial and learned gentleman with an enquiring mind, John later went on to earn a Bachelor of Arts degree and became a Methodist lay preacher. Aunt Rita married Peter Carey in 1953. Uncle Peter's work in farming had brought him to Cliffe with the Kent Land Corps. Before National Service he worked on Clare Batchelor's farm at Rye Street Cliffe with Karl Nushki a German POW, Dick and Desmond Batchelor (Clare's sons), Edwin Twittchett, Albert Martin, Ted Webdale (the Milkman), Billy Herby, Ronnie Gill, and Mike Sullivan.

Sheila talking to a neighbour while visiting her parents at Turner Street with a parcel under her arm. The parcel probably contained caps for her father. Every year, my granddad bought a new cap from Parker's. Sheila brought home 6 caps from Parker's for my granddad to try. Thereafter Sheila returned to Parker's with payment for the chosen cap and to return the other five caps.

During the war, Sheila lived at Millcroft Road and walked over to No 6 Turner Street every day to help her mum. Sheila had been in service, and this reflected in her housework: the house was always cleaned and tidied to perfection. Like so many families during the war, there would have been a sense of tense anticipation in Burton household. With family in military service, grandmother never locked the door at night in case one came home on leave unexpectedly. Tea was one commodity that was rationed in the war. After breakfast at her home in Millcroft Road, Sheila would go to the garden and pass the teapot over the fence to her neighbour Mrs White to make a brew from the used tea.

Of the war years, Jack Sullivan[10] recalled to me an interesting observation that he made toward the end of the war. He was working at the Alpha and happened to glance in the direction of the Thames Estuary; he saw a thin vapour trail rising rapidly above the distant horizon. Minutes later an explosion was heard. Sometime in the same period, my father[12] witnessed a similar event. On a clear morning in 1944, he was riding in a lorry through Strood and happened to be looking to the east when he saw a thin vapour trail rising rapidly over the horizon. The vapour trail broke into a zigzag pattern: he reasoned that this was due to high altitude wind speed differentials. Minutes later he heard in the distance the characteristic double bang of a V2 rocket impact. He estimated the impact was in the order of ten miles from Strood. My father had witnessed several V2 impacts at the end of the war. These were characteristic, comprising of an initial sonic boom followed by the warhead explosion. Both Jack Sullivan and my father had witnessed something of the coming age. From beyond the distant North Sea a rocket had ascended from the continent of Europe. Its trajectory was a huge arc that extended beyond our planet's atmosphere sending the rocket hundreds of miles across the earth within a matter of minutes. From a quiet corner of Kent in the mid 1940s, two people at least witnessed at first hand the embryonic work of the German engineer who would only 25 years later play an important role in sending men to the Moon.

My father originated from Chatham; he was the son of Albert and Winifred Tester. My father and my aunt Daphne were from an old Chatham family with roots in the Dockyard. My grandfather Albert served in the Navy during World War One, and after the war he worked in the ropery at the Dockyard. My father met my mother during the war when they both worked at the Uralite in Higham. Dad used to ride his bicycle over to Cliffe to visit my mum. One evening as he was en route to Cliffe anti-aircraft gunning started at the Dillywood Battery just as he neared the Stone Horse Pub. Shrapnel started to rain down around him. He lay on the ground with the bicycle on top of him "for all the good that would have done" as he later recalled. There was a lull in the firing so he proceeded on to Cliffe. That night there was a bombing raid so he decided to stay the night at No 6 Turner Street. During such raids, the family took cover by putting their heads under the large table in the downstairs front room. And that is how they slept that night. My dad woke up in the middle of the night as Madge came down the stairs in her dressing gown. On awaking to the sight of Madge, in gown of white and a cloth covering her head to cover her hair curlers, he thought the "angels had come". On the way back to Chatham that morning he picked up a large piece of shrapnel from the road near Dillywood. My mother kept that piece of shrapnel for years.

During the war a V1 flying bomb impacted on the field to the east of Turner Street. It had been intercepted and shot at by a British aircraft, downing the flying bomb. Its descent took it over the Morning Cross cottages before impacting in the field (Steve Holroyd via his granddad "Yorkie" Edwards). My mother was working at the Uralite at the time of the explosion, and on hearing the news the management sent the Cliffe workers home. On returning to Turner Street, she found the damage that the shock wave from the bomb had caused: some slates were missing from the roofs, and the internal walls of the Turner Street houses had yielded to the explosion. Strangely, the outer brick walls of the terrace were intact. Building materials in wartime Britain were limited so the council replaced the damaged internal walls with a heavy-duty paper material painted with distemper.

Bernard Martin recalled how the war affected the area around the northern end of Church Street and Reed Street: During the war a large oil bomb exploded in Soap Suds Alley next to Longford House destroying one house and covering all of the wooden houses in that location in oil. Luckily, serious fire was avoided for all of the associated incendiary bombs fell in the location of Red House and due eastwards to the Hatcher's back garden near Mr and Mrs Bett's orchard in Reed Street thus narrowly missing by yards all of the oil-soaked houses. Bernard recalled that a bomb fell straight down the chimney of a pair of houses destroying one house and leaving the other standing. Bernard recalled looking at the house that was still standing and seeing the scrape marks in the soot in the exposed half of the chimney where the bomb had scraped the sides on the way down.

Bernard Martin recalled another occasion when a very large bomb landed in the field that later became Swingate Avenue; it failed to explode. All of Reed Street and the nearby area were evacuated while the bomb was dealt with. Bernard recalled watching from an upstairs window as the bomb was being taken away on the back of a large lorry. The resulting excavation hole was not filled in, and for years after people dumped their rubbish in that hole. A few years after the war Swingate Avenue was built and a concrete road was laid. Soon after, the road began to sink over the location of that excavation hole. Some remedial work was required on that part of the road.

During the war, Aunt Sis was involved in medical duties. My mother can picture Aunt Sis to this day on her pushbike and uniform riding to Dillywood. Back in the old Francis Chalk Quarry some Cliffe residents took nightly shelter from the bombing raids, sleeping in the two caves of the chalk hill[2&5]. Eric Slater lived in the blacksmith's cave for a year during the war. He remembers the soot on the cave walls from the old blacksmith's fire[5]. The Army held practice manoeuvres in the Francis Chalk Quarry. Part of those manoeuvres involved an old army tank. After the war, the army tank was left near to the cliff on the most southerly part of the quarry. Topsoil from the excavation of the Alpha chalk pit at Salt Lane was tipped off over that cliff and into the Francis Chalk Quarry. Eventually this formed a steep bank that totally covered the army tank[1].

World War Two clothing ration coupon given to me by Aunt Sis.

Dick Dowsett recalls the Francis chalk and clay pits during his youth in the early 1940s. In the lake of the second mud hole stood the Dando wind pump. In the cold winter of 1941 or it might have been 1945 the lake froze over. Dick, his brother Bernie, Ray Francis and John Herby walked on the thick ice out to the Dando where they dared John Herby to climb up to the platform at the top of the wind pump. And he did climb up to the platform. Dick recalls that some of the redundant artefacts of the old Francis days were still in place: the iron delivery pipe from the Dando ran to a concrete channel on the bank. Via the sloping concrete channel, the water ran under gravity to the ditch along Creek Road. To this day that concrete channel remains in the meadow that lies between Creek Road and the second clay pit. Sat upon the railway lines that run into the second mud hole in Dick's youth was a pair of railway wheels. They had a game where they would push the wheels as far as possible up the line and set them rolling down into the lake. During the time of the Blitz, a family from Green Lane walked each evening to the blacksmith's cave in the Francis Chalk Quarry. In the cave was a shed in which they slept. Up on the chalk hill the water tank remained from the Francis days. The rusting tank was made of riveted iron sections, and there were just enough sections on a side for the letters FRANCIS to be painted on each section. The works name faced the direction of the river.

Dick recalls the summer months of his youth. After school the boys and girls often ran down to Cliffe Creek for a swim. At Ivy House there was a tap and an old chipped enamel cup on a chain where people passing by could get a drink. Groups of ten or twenty children often gathered at Cliffe Creek for swimming.

THE DUMMY AIRDROME

The structure built in the Second World War to house a generator for a dummy airdrome on Cliffe Marshes. It is located on the Point Road 150 yards south of Boatwick House. The building was never used for its intended purpose.

Photograph by Clive Tester April 2021

The following information regarding the dummy airdrome is courtesy of Dick Dowsett[11] whose father worked as a shepherd on the marshes:

The building in the above photograph had a concrete base for a generator and a trench into which wires were laid but not covered. In fact, this building was never used because it was later decided that it was in the wrong place. A second building was subsequently built a mile further east of this building on land owned by Edmunds. It had a curved corrugated steel frame covered with earth and a platform on the top with a domed red light and a hand-controlled search light. It had generators driven by a petrol engine and a separate room with 2 bunk beds. Two hundred yards north of that, running west to east, was a line of lights shielded to face just east. Two R.A.F Regiment personnel manned it at night and were both billeted in Reed Street: one with Miss Ayers and one with Miss Richards. After the war the building was demolished.

On the two-hundred-acre marsh shepherded by Dick's father two landmines fell of which one did not explode. Four large bombs also exploded. Eight unexploded fifty kilo bombs remain there to this day. A team of R.A.F Regiment tried to extract at least one but the side of the pit fell in overnight. Luckily no one was injured and the attempt to remove the bomb was abandoned. Two hundred incendiary bombs fell on the marshes and over half of those did not explode as the light bombs fell on soft ground. Dick's brother Bernard's job was to pull the incendiaries out of the ground and put them into a pile and ignite them. During the first two years of the war, Dick recalls that the petrol tanks across the river were often alight.

THE CEMENT FAMILIES OF CLIFFE

Along with my grandfather and my uncle Sid, Dave Wassell the husband of my aunt Fay worked at the Salt Lane works. The Burton family were one of many families for whom successive generations worked in the local cement industry. The Alpha was an important part of community life in Cliffe. The industry was very important economically to the families of Cliffe among them the Hatcher family:

Alan and Molly Hatcher at Creek Road around 1947. Note the industrial building on the right: it is on the site of the I.C Johnson cement works at the eastern end of the creek. Photograph courtesy of Adrian Hatcher.

To name but a few families with a long association with Cliffe cement making were the family Slater who featured in chapter 1, and the Hatcher family. The Hatcher family settled in Cliffe around the 1880s, and family members worked in the Victorian era cement works at Cliffe. Alan Hatcher, born in 1928, worked as a fitter at the Alpha from the 1940s until its closure in 1970. Alan and Molly Hatcher ran the Cliffe cubs for many years devoting much of their time to the cubs of which my generation of children greatly enjoyed. Their son Adrian took many of the photographs for this book, and with our friends of Cliffe Adrian spent many a boyhood day among the wild lands of Under the Hill.

Alan Hatcher (Left) on a crane at the Alpha in 1949. Photograph courtesy of Adrian Hatcher.

Among the current population of Cliffe residents are the children of Brian and Jill Arnold: Tracey Dockwray nee Arnold, David, Douglas and Duncan. The Arnold family can trace their ancestry back to 19th century Cliffe and its burgeoning cement industry. David and his siblings' great grandfather's family came to Cliffe from Scotland on a cement barge sometime in the 19th century. Their great grandfather worked in a quarry of olden Cliffe. David's Uncle Tom Bolton was a foreman of the Alpha during the 1950s and 60s[26].

Manual chalk diggers at Cliffe. The man on the left is Sidney McPherson the Great Granddad of Brian and Jill Arnold's children David, Douglas Duncan and Tracey. Photograph courtesy of Doug Arnold.

Sidney McPherson's retirement certificate. Courtesy of David Arnold.

My mother recalls of the 1930s that her father would frequently talk factory with Mr Harrison of Millcroft Road; Mr Harrison worked at the Alpha. Mr and Mrs Harrison had eight boys of whom Roy would later do many things for the village. Roy was a champion of the marshes and always concerned with their conservation. Up to the end of the 20th century, Roy did a lot for the children of Cliffe School. He took the children on walks around the Cliffe countryside, and also led the children in daffodil planting at the school.

Roy Harrison (at the right of the photograph), Arthur Meddows (centre) and John Burton (closest to the car) at Turner Street circa 1950. Photograph courtesy of John Burton.

The Martin family were one of many families who moved from Essex around the 1860s to work in Kent's growing cement industry[23]. Two Cliffe residents, Steve and David Martin, are of the current generation of the Martin family who owe their long association with Cliffe to the cement industry. Steve and David's great great grandfather George Martin was born in Belchamp St Pauls in the north of Essex in 1837. He appears on the Cliffe census in 1871 as a cement labourer living in Warf Lane with his wife Harriet and children. George had eight children; the eldest Edward Henry Martin worked as a cement labourer at Cliffe. Edward had ten boys and three girls, and most of Edward's sons worked as cement labourers at Cliffe. One of those ten boys was John "Jack" Martin. When Jack Martin married in 1932 he rented one of the Coast Guard Cottages. His son Bernard Martin was born in the Coastguard Cottages in 1933. Bernard, father of Steve and David, kept cement in his blood by becoming a master builder[23].

THE FAMILIES OF THE COASTGUARD COTTAGES.

The Coast Guard Cottages circa 1990. Situated on Cliffe Marshes close to Lower Hope Point, this row of cottages was once the home of many old Cliffe families including Tubby Slater and family, and the families Higglesden, Martin, Knight, Pennell, Ward, Harrison, Crayford and son Stan. Photograph courtesy of Steve Martin.

Handed down from father to son, it is said that the Coast Guard Cottages were built upon foundations of bundles of faggots[11]. Dick Dowsett remembers that Albert Slater and his family lived in the house nearest to the road, and in the next house lived George Slater and his family. They came to live there around the time when they started working on the pontoon cranes in this area around 1937. Janet Ledger recalls that George and Elsie Slater's son Eric married their next-door neighbour's daughter Ella Knight. Eric, like his father, went on to work on the pontoon cranes.

The Cliffe ancestry of Janet Keats[35] nee Brenchley extends back to the Curtis's and Harvey era. Janet's grandparents William and Beatrice Higglesden moved from the Isle of Grain to the Coastguard Cottages at Cliffe; William was night watchman at the munitions works. In the 1930s, Janet's mother Winifred Brenchley[36] nee Higglesden walked to school each day from the Coastguard Cottages[3]. When the Second World War broke out Winifred was around school leaving age, and from around 14 or 15 years of age worked at the Alpha chalk pit[35 & 36]. Winifred and others including Doff Reddick were given the task of searching for "Blue Eggs"[35 & 36]: these were chalk nodules of value, being of a purity that made them suitable for use in the cosmetics industry[35 & 36]. During the war, Winifred drove the locomotives at the Alpha. This involved driving a train laden with cement from the Alpha to the jetty by Cliffe Fort and returning with coal for the Alpha[35 & 36]. The Brenchley family moved from the Coastguard Cottages to a house in Millcroft Road in 1946 or 1947[3].

Audrey Ward nee Knight was the sister of Ella Pennell and the Coastguard Cottages was Ken and Audrey Ward's first marital home. The Ward family moved from the

Coastguard Cottages in July 1962 into Wadland's Road Cliffe the same day as the Pennell family moved from the Coastguards to Rookery Crescent Cliffe. The Ward family were one of the first families to move into the newly built Wadland's Road, and their house was brand new[27].

Penelope Harris nee Pennell recalls of her early childhood at the Coastguard Cottages in the late 1950s/early 1960s that Derek and Kath Green's dormobile service would provide the school run from the Coastguard Cottages and the Creek. Derek and Kath would pick up the school children from the Coastguard Cottages and then drive round to Cliffe Creek to collect the children of the Madden family.

Coastguard Cottages were home to Mr and Mrs Crayford and their son Stan; Stan became a postman. My mother recalls when Stan's mother told her that Stan was to work for the Post Office: my mother asked if Stan was going to work behind the counter to which Mrs Crayford replied "Oh no, he would lick the stamps and stick them to the customer's face." Indeed, Stan Crayford was a natural comedian, and he was a professional children's entertainer. He provided entertainment at Pauline and Terry Springhall's wedding at Cliffe memorial Hall in 1969. I recall Stan, as a postman of Cliffe in the 1970s and 80s, as being a very good natured and jovial man who was very popular with the local children. When he came to collect the post from the post box outside my mother's post office at Church Street, the children would gather round to see him perform a ventriloquist act: pretending that someone was locked in the letter box and making earnest calls for help. On one snowy day, a group of children followed his van along Church Street while pelting his van with snowballs; something that Stan had clearly anticipated. Stan stopped his van at a certain point in the road where he had earlier assembled a pile of snowballs. He quickly got out and started throwing the snowballs back at the crowd of children. On Stan's retirement in the early 1990s he was presented at Cliffe Post Office with a "This is your life" book prepared by my parents.

Cliffe resident Peter Knight recalled for this book his family's long association with Lower Hope Point. On Peter Knight's maternal side of the family, granddad Harold Loveland worked at the Curtis's and Harvey explosives factory at Lower Hope Point. Peter's paternal grandfather Herbert Knight also worked at the Curtis's and Harvey explosives factory. Herbert Knight was a foreman at the factory during its operation, and when the factory closed he became the watchman of the site. Peter's father Herbert Knight later took over watchman's duties. Many memories from the time when the munitions works was in operation have been passed down in the family's memories. For example, Mr Bently used to hire pushbikes out of his bicycle shop at 195 Church Street for folk to ride to work at the explosives factory. During the Second World War, Herbert junior had the task of putting lights on the two former Curtis's and Harvey jetties; these were specialised lights that did not shine upwards. The Knight family lived in 2 bungalows on the Curtis's and Harvey site. During the war a landmine was dropped nearby and damaged the bungalows. The Knight family had to move into the Coastguard Cottages. Later the family moved back to the bungalows after repairs. During the Second World War, the Port of London Authority held their documents at the former Curtis's and Harvey site: documents that were normally kept in London. Peter recalls the 1953 flood: sheep were able to seek refuge from the floodwaters on the many earth mounds of the munitions works.

CHAPTER 3

THE DAYS OF THE ALPHA

THE ALPHA, AN OVERVIEW

Construction of the cement factory at Salt Lane Cliffe began in 1910, and the factory was opened in 1913[1]. The Factory was built by the Thames Portland Cement Co. Ltd[1]. The reception building of the works remained in place for some years after the factory's demolition in the late 1970s, and the building sported a plaque which read: *"Thames Portland Cement Co. Ltd 1913"* [22]. To the age group who remembered the Victorian era cement factories at Cliffe, which ceased production in 1921, the cement factory at Salt Lane was known colloquially as "The New Factory"[1].

Initially, the Salt Lane cement factory was under the ownership of the Thames Portland Cement Company, and throughout its 60-year history ownership of the factory changed several times. In 1934 the factory was acquired from Thames Portland Cement by the Alpha Group[14 & 15]. As recalled by Stan Beeching[14], there was a strong Danish influence to the Alpha Group who ran the factory. Many of the electric motors used at the Alpha bore the company logo FLS, a Danish company[14]. Stan recalls that during a period in Alpha ownership a Dane, Peder Moller[14&35] was the Works Manager. The Moller family had some significant roles at the factory and in the village: Peder Moller's daughter was secretary at the Alpha[35], and his son went on to be the village doctor[35] around the period of the 1960s[3].

In 1938 the Alpha Group was taken over jointly by the APCM and Tunnel Cement, and wholly by the APCM in 1948[15]. Though the retirement certificate given to my grandfather as shown in chapter 2 bears the Alpha Cement Limited logo, and this certificate dates from 1949 or 1950 around a decade after the takeover. Indeed, as far as operations at the factory were concerned, the factory remained within the remit of the Alpha until the early 1950s as recalled by Stan Beeching: Documentation produced at the factory bore the Alpha logo up until the early 1950s[14]. *The Alpha* as a term for the Salt Lane cement works and its associated quarries has remained firmly within the village vernacular to this day.

Initially the factory produced clinker from a single rotary kiln; a second rotary kiln was added in the mid 1920s[21]. In the factory's early period under Thames Portland cement, chalk and clay digging and cement packing were manual tasks; these were later replaced by mechanical means[14]. Under the ownership of the Alpha from 1934, the factory was upgraded: Number 1 kiln was replaced with a kiln of the same length but of greater circumference, while number 2 kiln was not replaced[14]. Both kilns were fitted with calcinators that nodulized the slurry before it entered the kiln[14]. The result of adding the calcinators was an increase in the clinker output[14]. However, the addition of the calcinators created a dust nuisance for the local area at Cliffe and in local agriculture affecting among other things a tulip farm and Newland's Nurseries greenhouses[14]. Later the calcinators were removed and the kilns returned to a wet feed method with chains being added to the cold end of the kilns[14]. A third kiln was added in 1936[14]. The third kiln was of greater length and of greater output than the earlier two, and it employed a wet feed method[14]. Stan Beeching helped to pour the concrete for the third kiln's concrete chimney[14].

To mitigate the dust problem, electrostatic precipitators were added to all three kilns; though these sometimes tripped out[14]. Dust collected from the precipitators was conveyed to the clay lake to the north of the factory adjacent to Fort Road via a narrow concrete channel; the dust was mixed and carried with waste water from the grinding mill room[14].

Stan Beeching enjoyed a long career at the Alpha. Hitherto he had been a farm worker, but one day in 1936 he waited outside of the gates of the Alpha with a group of many other men who were hoping for work at the factory that day. No call for work came, and most of the group went home. Only Stan and one other man remained and their perseverance paid off: that day the two of them were taken on with temporary employment. Stan would go on to work at the Alpha until its closure in 1970[14]. Stan started at the Alpha as a general worker and worked on the construction of the railway lines at Fort Road and in the quarries. After war service from 20th May 1940 to 3rd March 1946 he worked on the chalk quarry excavator and later was quarry foreman then shift production foreman[14]. From 1970 to 1980, Stan was Whiting Plant foreman at Swanscombe until his retirement in 1980. Stan recalls that the Alpha was a boon for the area. Many people who were out of work got jobs at the factory and its associated quarries. With much overtime available, workers were going home with big wage packets. By the mid 1930s, around 300 people were employed at the site. Stan recalls of the earlier history of the works, when the factory was operating two kilns, that clinker output was little more than 400 to 450 tons per 24 hours. However, the factory could only operate one kiln at a time due to insufficient electrical power at the factory. The factory under Thames Portland Cement generated its own electricity by means of a steam engine which had its own small chimney[10 & 14]. The operation of the two kilns was rotated such that necessary maintenance could be performed on the kiln that was not in operation. The issue of limited electrical power at the factory was solved when the factory was connected to the mains electricity grid in 1929. Stan recalls that the factory used coal to fire the kilns; later over concerns about coal supply they changed temporarily to oil. The oil was of the thick fuel oil type that was like gel at room temperature. It had to be pre-heated before it went into the kiln. If the flame of a kiln went out they had to clear the set oil from the kiln lance. Sometimes they had to replace the lance if the oil set in the lance. Oil was transported to the factory via Everard's Transport from Northfleet or Swanscombe and stored in the "oil farm" at the rear of the factory[14]. With three kilns operating at the site, cement output was at a rate of 1000 tons per 24 hours.

A document relating to the Employees Profit Sharing Bonus Scheme which operated at the Cliffe cement works. Dated December 1947, it bears the Alpha Cement Limited name. Courtesy of Stan Beeching.

Viewed from the second Alpha pit the tanks of the oil farm are on the right. Note the conveyer belt traversing the chalk pit. This was used to convey cement from the clinker shed to a railway silo which was constructed in 1960 (detailed below). The railway silo remained, long after the cement works had gone, a familiar landmark on the Cliffe skyline until its demolition on March 16th 2021. Photograph by Clive Tester 1979.

Cement was not the only product produced at the factory. A by-product of the extraction of chalk, flint, was sent hundreds of miles away to the potteries to be used in the production of ceramics[1]. Aunt Sis was among the women who were employed at the factory to pick out the flints from chalk that had been brought to the factory from the quarries. In return, the potteries used to send pottery "seconds" down to the Cliffe factory. Employees could buy this slightly defective crockery for a low price. I recall, on my frequent visits to Aunt Sis, Quarry Cottages having a few examples of pottery sold at the factory.

Transportation of cement from the factory, to the Thames a little over a mile to the north, was in the early years of the factory via a Goshead aerial cableway [18]. At the Warf, cement was loaded onto barges. In return, coke destined for the kilns of the factory was loaded from barges onto the cableway[18]. The cableway was replaced with a narrow-gauge railway in 1935[18]. For more information on the Alpha's narrow-gauge railway system see Appendix B. Remnants of the old aerial cableway are still in evidence today. The bases of several of the cableway pylons exist in the lake to the north of the Alpha[5]. The lake is used today for boating, and the pylon bases are marked with bright orange floats[5].

In 1960, a new cement silo with loading facilities was constructed to the south of the Alpha to facilitate the despatch of cement via railway[10]. A branch line from the new silo to the Hundred of Hoo Railway at Lower Higham was opened in 1961[18]. The cement wagons were destined for Uddingston, and the train always departed from Cliffe in the early morning hours[14].

The Alpha in its final configuration in the 1960s. Photograph by Albert Smith courtesy of Martyn Smith.

The photograph above was taken from West Street Cliffe in the 1960s by Albert Smith who worked at the Alpha. The three silo buildings are present from left to right: The railway silo; The block of six silos five of which were used to contain ordinary cement and one used for rapid hardening cement[14]; The tallest of the silo blocks consisted of two silos which contained 1200 tons of cement each[14]. Local accounts recalled in my diary from the 1970s record that the set of six silos were known locally as silo 1 and the set of two silos as silo 2. My diary records that the set of two silos at the right of the picture were built in the mid 1930s in the place of two old cottages.

The three Alpha chimneys were 165 feet, 180 feet and 200 feet tall[14]. The smallest chimney was constructed for the kiln which was added in 1936[14]. It was of concrete construction and Stan Beeching helped to pour the concrete during its construction[14].

As of 2015, the corrugated iron engine shed (also called the fitting shed) at the northern end of the old Alpha site that served the narrow-gauge railway system was still in place. Within the shed, the narrow-gauge railway lines were still in evidence.

This photograph was taken from the junction of Fort Road and Salt Lane following the demolition of the smallest chimney of the Alpha. The engine shed can be seen behind the fallen chimney.

Photograph by Clive Tester February 1980.

Me in the Alpha engine shed in 1991.

AN EXPLOSION AT THE ALPHA. RECALLED BY STEVE HOLROYD, GRANDSON OF JAMES EDWARDS.

James Edwards was born in 1892 and came to Cliffe around 1938 having worked at Betteshanger colliery in Kent after leaving his home county of Yorkshire; he was known as Yorky in his adopted southern home. A veteran of the Great War, he also took part in the allied intervention force sent to Russia following the 1917 revolution. One of the memories he related of the Russian tour was that in the cold winter, his army unit had to sleep under canvass. He once made the mistake of taking his boots off to sleep and found in the morning that his boots were frozen stiff and consequently very difficult to put on.

His grandson, Steve Holroyd remembers as a four-year-old boy in 1954 riding on the front basket of his grandfather's bicycle to the cement works where Yorky worked as a kiln burner. As a boy, Steve would often go with his grandfather to the factory at Salt Lane. He remembered that there was a raised walkway between the rotary kilns, and that during their operation the radiated heat from the kilns was almost unbearably intense.

Steve remembered as a boy hearing a great commotion outside of his house late one night and banging on the door. Staff from the cement works took Yorky away in a car to the cement factory. A coal powder explosion had occurred at the cement factory and all employees including Yorky were needed to help in the aftermath. Apparently, the flame in the rotary kiln had flashed back along the kiln lance and into the bulk of the coal powder causing the coal handling system to explode. A few days after the coal dust explosion Steve saw that the force of the explosion had blown much of the back of the kiln hall out; corrugated iron sheets were strewn across the football field that lay behind the factory.

CLAY FOR THE ALPHA AND SWANSCOMBE

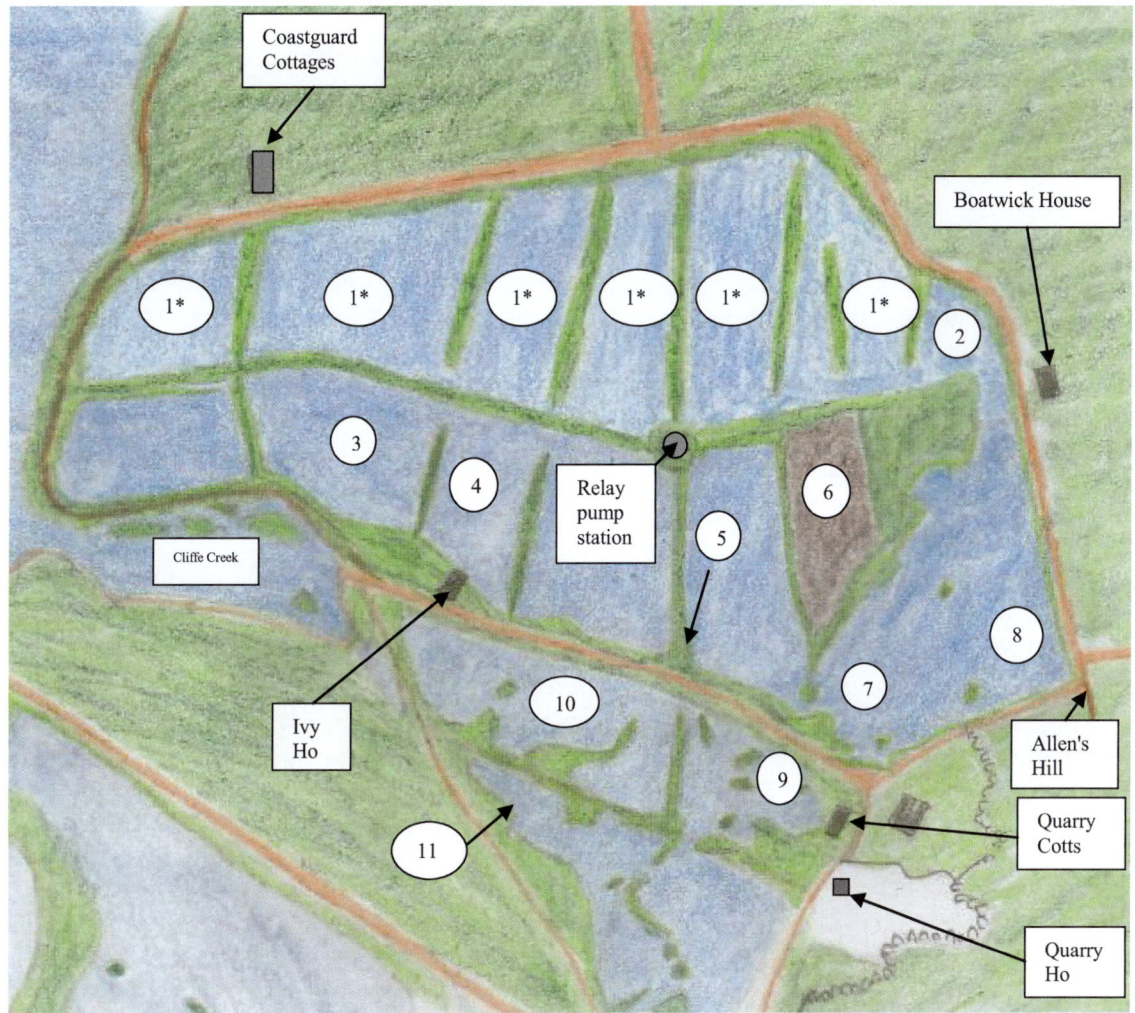

Notations 1 to 11 are the original names of the clay lakes as known by the men who worked on the lakes. The information for this map was provided by Gill Moore from information provided by pontoon crane operators Dick Dowsett and Eric Slater, and *local historian Robert Hutchings.

KEY:-

1*: The Polders. These lakes were filled in with river dredgings in the 1960s to the 1970s. Respected local historian Robert Hutchings named this area the Polders after similar land in Holland.

2: Moldie's Lake was named after Fred "Moldie" Gulvin who was a shepherd at Boatwick House.

3: Sluice. Named after the sluice that runs to Cliffe Creek from this lake.

4: Joe's Lake. Named after Joe Caller who lived at Ivy House and kept goats which grazed at the ruins of the old cement works.

5: The Bundy. The lake was named after the clocking in/off machine that was called the Bundy and was situated in the area where the arrow is pointing on the map. I recall that the clocking machine was still in place up to the late 1970s.

6: The Dry Digger. A dry method of clay extraction was used for this pit. Material was transported from the pit via a conveyor belt. The method was not very successful as the belt often clogged, and constant pumping of water out of the lake was required.

7: The Dando. Named after the Dando wind pump that stood in this area. This area was the original clay pit referred to as the second mud hole in chapter 1.

8: Allen's Hill Lake.

9: The Kingfisher. This area was the original clay pit referred to as the first mud hole in chapter 1.

10: Opposite Joes. Named because it was opposite Joe' Lake.

11: Shepherd's Wick. The lake was named after a shepherd's wick hut that sat on the western bank of the lake.

During the early years of the operation of the factory, clay for cement production was excavated from a dry pit to the north of the works adjacent to the Fort Road[2&14]. Stan Beeching and Sid Burton recalled that the clay pit to the north of the factory was initially hand dug. Stan recalls that clay was brought from the pit via a narrow-gauge railway on a rope pulley system. The chalk pits to the south and west of the factory operated with a similar narrow-gauge railway that was on a rope pulley system.

When the Alpha took management of the works in 1934, the clay pit to the north of the Alpha was flooded to accommodate a new method of clay extraction by cranes that were floated on pontoons. Clay that was dug from the lake in this manner was liquefied with water and pumped via a floating pipeline to the works. The pontoon cranes operated with a crew of two, which consisted of the crane driver and a wash mill attendant [14].

From the late 1920s, clay from Cliffe marshes was also sent further afield to cement works that operated in higher regions of the tidal Thames including Swanscombe[1]. Stan Beeching recalls that in 1928/1929 a call went out for men to dig a clay pit at Point Road. This operation was under the remit of the APCM[14]. The purpose of the pit was to accommodate a pontoon crane which would supply clay to Swanscombe and the other works on the Thames. Stan's father helped to dig the pit. When the pit was large enough it was filled with water. From that time until 1966[1], the fields to the north and west of Allen's Hill were dug by use of pontoon cranes to form the lakes that are known to my generation as the Pontoons. Sid Burton and Richard Filmer recalled the time when what is now the lake at the bottom of Allen's Hill was a pasture where cattle used to graze. The cattle used to be led along Allen's Hill to Allen's Hill Farm for milking.

Aunt Sis recalled that in 1938, the lake that had formed in the second mud hole was drained of its water. The water was probably required to fill one of the new pontoon lakes nearby. Artefacts including a workman's shed at the bottom of that clay pit were visible for the first time in decades.

A pontoon crane operating to the north of Allen's Hill in 1938. This photograph was given to me by Aunt Sis on my 13th birthday. Aunt Sis wrote on the back of this photograph:" Given to Clive Aug 21st 1978 from M Hoare".

Eric Slater and Dick Dowsett were among the men who worked on the pontoon cranes and they have a wealth of memories of that time in the marsh's history:

Eric Slater recalled that working on the cranes was sometimes difficult in a strong wind. As each bucket load of clay was brought from the depths wringing wet, a shower of muddy water would be blown onto the windscreen of the crane cab making it impossible to see even with the wipers. Each bucket was placed into the wash mill where it was liquidised and pumped into the pipeline. The pressure of the pumps was set at 80 psi. Eric recalls that ancient pottery and other artefacts were sometimes brought up with the clay. They once found pottery of hare and leaf patterns that was brought up from the Pontoons. The clay layer into which the crane dug varied in depth. Near the Coastguard Cottages and the area adjacent to Boatwick House the clay layer was only about 10 feet thick with sand underneath. In other places the clay layer went down as far as the cables on the crane could go. At the clay lake to the south of the Alpha on Higham Marshes, when they dug beneath the clay layer, they brought up peat composed of reeds and the peat floated. When dried the peat could be burned.

The pontoon crane on Higham Marshes used for the Cliffe works. Richard Tester is in the photograph; he is the great grandson of Alpha employee Ernest Burton. Photograph by Clive Tester 2002.

Dick Dowsett remembers excavating clay from the lake immediately to the north of Black Path. From under the clay layer they brought up chalk pebbles and also compressed sand. In this location they brought up the planks of a boat and also pottery and coins.

Aunt Sis recalled that the pontoon crane once brought up a large fossilised tree trunk. It was placed on the bank near to the relay pump station: the fossilised trunk could not be cut with a saw. Gradually the fossilised trunk slipped back into the lake and remains there to this day. Aunt Sis recalled that the relay pump station was built in 1950. Dick Dowsett recalls that before the introduction of the relay pump station, clay was pumped directly from the cranes to the distribution point at the sea wall. But as clay lakes were excavated further from the Thames, a relay pump was required.

The relay pump station used to pump liquefied clay from the pontoon cranes to the sea wall; it operated from 1950 to 1966[1]. Note the Coastguard Cottages in the lower picture. Photographs by Clive Tester 1989.

Of the creek and surrounding area during the time of the pontoon cranes, Dick Dowsett remembers that goats and sheep were kept on the field to the east of Fort Road, and Joe Caller of Ivy House kept goats around the area of the Creek. There was a post box at Ivy house up to the 1960s as recalled by Dick Dowsett and Sid Burton. Sid remembered the postman Sid Sherlock used to ride to Ivy House on his bike to collect the post. Then he would leave his bike at Ivy House and walk over to the Coastguard Cottages to deliver their post. Sid Sherlock lodged at the houses near the Evening Star Pub in Cliffe. Dick remembers of his days operating the pontoon crane in the lake to the south of Ivy House Joe Caller's evening routine. Joe took his dog for a walk at 9pm every night, and the light in Ivy House always went out at 9.10pm shortly after Joe's return. My mother remembers Joe Caller as an interesting character. He was a keen stamp collector and he used to buy sheets of first edition stamps at the post office: the stamps had to be in pristine condition for Joe. Joe also made models of ships which were immaculately constructed. With the demolition of Ivy House, Mr and Mrs Caller moved to Quarry Cottages.

In the early 1950s, Creek Road was breached in order to transfer the pontoon crane between the Bundy and the Kingfisher lakes. Dick and Eric observed the profile of the old canal when the road was cut through. The place where the road was breached can be discerned to this day where there is a slight dip in Creek Road near to the site of the old yacht club[1].

The manner in which clay was extracted with the pontoon cranes meant that the water level in the clay lakes had to be maintained. Because the clay was mixed with water from the lake and pumped out to the factory, the displaced water needed replenishment. Water was pumped into the lakes from the well in the western end of the Francis chalk pit[1 & 17]. Water was also sourced from the Black Lane well[1&11] a little way to the east of quarry cottages (Refer to the map at the end of chapter 1). An 1870 ordnance survey map shows a house on the site of that well, but during Aunt Sis' memory only the well remained. In more recent times, the well was capped with a concrete top which is visible today. Another source of water for the clay lakes was from a well immediately in front of the arches at the western side of the Francis Chamber Kiln[11]. Water from the Black Lane well was pumped to Dando Lake via a pipe over a bank of quarry topsoil that lies between Black Lane and the Dando Lake; the bank was known locally as Lover's Bank[11]. Water from the two Francis Chalk Quarry sources was pumped into a ditch at the southern most end of Creek Road. Each source ran via troughs with V-notch flow indicators before entering the lake or ditch[11]. This was because payment was due to the water company for water extracted from the wells[11]. A galvanised steel hut sat over each of the wells housing an electric water pump[11]. The electric water pumps ran night and day, and during the eight years that Dick Dowsett worked on the pontoon cranes he never knew of them requiring maintenance. These water sources fed into the lakes north of Creek Road. So that water would reach the lakes to the south of Creek Road, a pipe was laid under Creek Road[11]. The pipe is in the area of Creek Road that was once breached to transfer the pontoon crane between the Bundy and the Kingfisher lakes[11]. At one time this pipe became blocked, and the cement company arranged for divers to go down and inspect it. The divers were in old style diving suits[11].

Where the water flowed into the ditch at Creek Road, watercress was cultivated. My brother Victor Tester and brother in law Steve Holroyd recall during their childhood in the 1960s that the water, which emerged from the iron pipe, was clear and cool and of sufficient quality to drink. Although there was, as Victor recalls, a sign on the water pipe stating: "Do not drink the water". Steve and Victor also recall that there were many newts in the ditch. A part of that iron water pipe was still in evidence at the end of Creek Road into the first decade of the 21st century.

Dick Dowsett described for this book the power arrangement for the pontoon cranes. The pontoon cranes were powered by 110- volt DC transformed from 240-volt mains AC at a substation that was likely situated at the eastern end of Cliffe Creek. A mains overhead power line ran from the field behind what is now the Vicar's house on Church Street Cliffe. It ran to the direction of Manor Farm and along Black Path to the direction of Quarry Cottages. From there it ran along the path that was the old tramway adjacent to Shepherds Wick Lake and on to Cliffe Creek. From the substation at the creek, 110-volt DC power was transmitted through a heavily armoured land cable across the marshes to the cranes.

During the 1960s, a method of extracting clay by use of a dry digging machine was used on a limited scale in a clay pit situated to the north of Allen's hill and to the west of Boatwick House. The pit, which was known to the clay digger operators as the Dry Digger, was kept dry by use of a water pump, and today forms a small lake. The digging machine was mounted on rails which ran adjacent to the edge of the pit[28].

Remains of machinery by the Dry Digger pit.

Photograph by Clive Tester 1991.

THE BOMBING OF THE PONTOON CRANE

Of the many bombs that were dropped by German aeroplanes over the Cliffe area during World War Two, one was particularly relevant to the production at the Alpha and to an industrial relic that survives to this day. The register for air raids and alarms[9] for Cliffe, dated 5th June 1943, shows that a single 500-kilogram high explosive bomb was dropped at 02.05 hours; the location was stated as the Alpha cement works Cliffe. Services that were put out of action were the factory electricity supply; the description of buildings damaged was stated as follows: -

Pontoon sunk, pipeline damaged, electricity and windows. Extensive damage to excavator and pumping plant Alpha cement factory, which will entail loss of output for some time. Slight damage to three houses in vicinity.

Both Jack Sullivan who worked as an engineer at the Alpha during the war, and Dick Dowsett whose father worked for James Edmonds & Sons the farmer who farmed the land to the east of Fort Road in that period, recalled to me the bombing of the pontoon crane. This particular pontoon crane was operating at the clay lake to the west of Fort Road. It was not directly hit, but shrapnel from the bomb sunk the crane. The crane was later re-floated. Dick recalled that in the mean time clay that was originally destined for the Swanscombe works was diverted from a pontoon crane operating in a lake near to Cliffe Creek. A pipe was laid that ran from a location near to Cliffe Creek to a building that was specially constructed following the bombing. This building was located by a ditch in the field immediately to the east of Fort Road, and it housed a pump. The ditch, on the bank of which this pumping station sat, was blocked off at its easterly end so that liquid clay could be stored there and later pumped to the Alpha via the truncated pipe of the sunken crane.

The Alpha and the clay lake to the west of Fort Road with a pontoon crane at the right. Photograph of unknown local origin taken after 1938.

The remains of the clay pumping station constructed following the bombing of the Alpha in June 1943. It lies in the field to the east of Fort Road. Photograph by Clive Tester 2014.

The field shown in the photograph above lies to the east of Fort Road and has at its eastern border the County Wall. Dick Dowsett recalled his memories of this field as it was in the 1940s: The fleet that flows through that field was of fresh water to part way along the County Wall whereupon the fresh water flowed into a part of the fleet that was tidal as it was connected to the creek. Local people often used to place a barrel with holes in it in front of the water flow to catch eels. Up until the start of World War Two, the field was composed of thick beds of reeds; it was a wet and marshy area. During World War Two, the field was ploughed and linseed was planted.

CHALK FOR THE ALPHA

The Alpha in 1938. Reproduced courtesy of the British Geological Survey IPR/183-56CN

The other primary constituent of cement, chalk, was initially taken from a pit approximately to the west of the factory. It should be noted that nothing is visible of the first chalk pit today; it was land filled long before the closure of the factory[31]. In the factory's early period, chalk was dug by hand, but while still under the ownership of Thames Portland Cement this method was superseded with a steam powered excavator[14]. Stan Beeching recalls that Horace Weedon was an operator of the steam powered excavator. From the 1930s onward, the following Ruston Bucyrus excavators were used: RB37 (diesel), RB48 (electric), RB54 (electric)[14].

When the first chalk pit became exhausted, a second pit was started to the south of the factory; this is the pit that is shown in the above photograph. The narrow-gauge railway shown in this photograph runs to a third pit that was excavated to the east of the road leading to West Court Farm. A 1934 map shows the third pit to be well established with a tunnel under the road to West Court Farm. In 1936 a second tunnel linking the second and third pits was bored to maintain railway connections with the factory as the third pit became deeper[2]. A decision to dig the third quarry deep, and ultimately below the water table, meant that the second tunnel was at a considerably lower level than the first. The first tunnel is brick lined through its entire span[14], and today a section of narrow gauge railway line is still present in the first tunnel[22]. The lower tunnel is of brick construction at the ends only[14], and today it is flooded. Sid Burton recalled that the depth of the third pit reached a point where the chalk became so hard that it was not practical to dig any further down.

It is interesting to note that when Stan Beeching started work at the Alpha in 1936, the removal of the overburden of soil, the top soil covering the chalk layer, was a manual task performed by a gang of men with shovels. It was required to remove the overburden from the chalk layer before quarrying could begin. Stan recalls my grandfather Ted Burton once taking a large urn of tea over to the gang of men who were removing the overburden. On the way my grandfather gave Stan a cup of tea from the urn. Later the removal of the overburden was performed by mechanical means. The machine that was later used for overburden removal was of great benefit to the village of Cliffe during the harsh winter of 1963 as Don Moore[34] recalls: The roads of Cliffe became completely impassable due to heavy snow. The Alpha used the top soil removal machine to clear the snow from the roads.

Evidence of the war years lays in the second and third chalk pits. These quarries have what appears to be concrete lined air raid shelters built into the chalk face of each pit. In addition, a part-buried structure a few tens of meters to the north of the Royal Albert Pub on Salt Lane was a World War Two air raid shelter[14]. Within this shelter lies a concrete plinth upon which during war time was fixed a bicycle operated air pump used to circulate air within the bunker[14]. A square concrete structure is in evidence on top of the tallest silo (Silo Number 2) in the 1960s photograph of the Alpha on page 71 and also in the photograph of the silo's demolition in chapter 4. This structure is absent from the 1938 photograph on page 80. This suggests a war related structure, perhaps a lookout post, had been added sometime after 1938. My memories of Silo Number 2 before its demolition include what appeared to be a large searchlight mounted on a walkway near the top of the silo.

The lower tunnel under the road to West Court Farm linking the second and third Alpha chalk pits.
Photograph by Clive Tester 1984.

By 1950, the third pit became exhausted and a fourth pit was started to the north of Salt Lane. In the 1950s, a tunnel was dug under Salt Lane between the third and fourth pits to maintain railway connections with the factory via the older pits. The job of building the tunnel was given to the *heavy gang*: employees of the Alpha who specialised in heavy manual work[1]. Three men dug the tunnel using a pneumatic drill and shovels; these were my uncle Perce Springhall, and two others known as Geordie and Paddy[2]. As the tunnel digging progressed under Salt Lane, the narrow-gauge railway line was extended to the tunnel face; the chalk diggings were removed in railway trucks[2]. The Salt Lane tunnel is lined inside with netting spayed with concrete, and its ends are of brick construction[14].

Dug by Perce, Geordie and Paddy in the 1950s: the tunnel beneath Salt Lane linking the third and fourth chalk pits. In the centre of the photograph some sticks are visible above the water which are the remains of the silver birch wood that once covered the bottom of the quarry.
Photograph by Clive Tester 1984.

IN MEMORY OF LIVES LOST

During the period of 1934 to 1940, four men lost their lives while working at the factory, these were[14]:

Ted Geer who was calcinator dust elevator attendant and died after being engulfed in hot dust while working in the calcinator elevator pit.
Charlie Hoare who was a cement packing plant greaser and died after being caught in the cement conveyer screw.
Bert Richards who was chalk quarry excavator Banksman and died after being crashed by a chalk fall in the chalk quarry. Locomotive driver Ted Morrad was injured in the same accident.
Ted Morrad: A year after his injury in the chalk fall, Ted Morrad was killed when his locomotive ran over him in the chalk quarry.

Our thoughts must go out to those who lost their lives in these tragedies, and to the families of those people.

THE END OF AN ERA

My older siblings recall of their summer walks to Salt Lane in the 1960s passing the cement silos of the Alpha and waving to Uncle Sid who would often be working on top of the silos. Sid was naturally generous to his extended family. As children we would often meet him riding his bicycle through the elder and sloe bordered paths Under the Hill. Sid would always stop and produce a coin from his pocket to give to us. My uncle Sid worked at the Alpha from the end of World War Two until the factory's closure along with his brother in law Perce Springhall. Sid remembers that during the 1953 flood, Perce of the Alpha heavy gang was in his element rescuing stranded sheep from the marsh adjacent to the factory. Perce had no problem in lifting a sheep in both arms and taking it to dry land. Perce once related to me of a time when a kiln broke down at the Alpha. Some of the firebricks that lined the inside of the kiln had come loose and fell away; the iron outer casing in that section of the kiln glowed red hot! Back in the 1930s, that would have been an occasion for my granddad to be called to the Alpha to help with the repairs. To all, granddad was known as Ted except for big genial Perce who always called him Teddy. Uncle Perce was down to earth and good-natured. He kept an immaculate garden; the furrows of his potato rows were neatly straight and deeply dug just like his tunnel that will always remain under Salt Lane. Perce had an eye for the simple aesthetics of a job well done.

On April 1st 1970, the Alpha closed [1 & 2]. There was a company flag on a pole near to the gates of the factory; gates that would soon close forever. Uncle Sid and a colleague lowered the flag to half-mast as an impromptu gesture to the last day of cement production at Cliffe. The chalk quarry remained in operation for a little longer for flint to be extracted for the potteries[1]. And there was talk in the village of the Alpha re opening with the possibility of the installation of a single rotary kiln in the fourth chalk pit[2]. Yet this never came to pass. I recall my aunt Madge coming around to 5 Rookery Crescent one afternoon with some big news in the village: the quarry was closing. The chalk pit was finally closed in 1972[1].

For over a century the cement industry of Cliffe had provided its men and women with local employment such that they were within walking distance of their work. Folk riding to work on cement-covered bicycles was a familiar sight in Cliffe. The redundancy money that the Alpha workers received softened the blow. For most the redundancy payout was the largest sum of money they had ever received in one lump. Many opened accounts with the newly introduced Post Office Investment Account. And many of those people found employment in the newly opened cement factory at Northfleet and in the lime and cement factories of the Medway: Martin Earl's lime works at Cuxton and the cement works of Halling and Snodland.

By the early 1970s, shortly after the closure of the Alpha, there remained within the Alpha chalk pits poignant reminders of industry past. Amid young Silver Birch trees lay rusting locomotives and wagons, and within a shed deep within the second quarry blue overalls and newspapers[16] left by those who had once made a living at the Alpha. The very spirit of that industry lay preserved in static isolation within the steep cliffs of the chalk pits. And within those pits existed a little world of the olden days of industrial Cliffe. It was a world where the chalky soil retained the memory of the heavy iron diggers this land once bore in deep furrows that soon became filled by wild flowers. It was a world where hogweed and willow grew quietly between the narrow-gauge railway lines of that industry passed; a world soon to be hidden forever beneath quiet waters.

Locomotives and railway wagons in the third Alpha pit in 1969 or 1970. Photograph by Dave Willis.

A locomotive and railway wagon in the third Alpha pit in 1969 or 1970. Photograph by Dave Willis.

Peter Knight at Salt Lane in 1969. Concrete Cottages and The Royal Albert pub are dwarfed by the silos and chimneys of the cement works. Photograph courtesy of Bob Knight.

The fourth Alpha pit in 1969. Photograph by Bob Knight.

CHAPTER 4

THE DAYS OF CHALK AND DRAGONFLIES

A BOYHOOD AMID A POST-INDUSTRIAL LANDSCAPE

The third Alpha pit in 1938. Reproduced courtesy of the British Geological Survey IPR/183-56CN

To my eye, the quarries of Cliffe add a wonderfully curious dimension to our land. They convey to me a sense of space and of distance that is altogether timeless. And I believe that this sense of timelessness is born of the mineral for which the quarries were excavated: the quarries were dug deep down into the strata of our distant past for chalk that was born of an era far removed from the age in which we now live and know. There is a pristine quality to the chalk beneath our land: it possesses a pureness that speaks of a time closer to our beginnings.

For me too, the process for which our quarries were created holds an allure that is akin I believe to the fascination many hold for the era of the steam locomotives. For there is a dynamism associated with the cement industry. It is dynamism embodied in the sparky rich aroma of burning coal; it is a dynamism born of the infernal heat of its kilns; it is a dynamism manifest in towering chimneys of billowing white steamy smoke ascending forth to the sky. The photograph above captures the essence of all that I found fascinating about the industry that shaped the landscape of our village.

I would pass this way a little over thirty years after this photograph was taken. And my experience of that day, of the quietly hidden legacy of our cement industry, shaped my perception of the industrial landscape of our village. With the promise of waterfalls, my brother Clifford took me to this quarry in the summer of 1970 or 1971. By our time in the early 1970s this quarry was yet deeper and its railway lines had long fallen silent. A silver birch wood had established at the end of the quarry from where these photographs had been taken.

The daisy sprinkled path that led down into this quarry seemed to take us so much further than the few short steps that it was from the hot thundering tarmac of Salt Lane. We walked through the silver birch wood while the faint sound of running water fuelled my growing sense of wonder for this mysterious place. Emerald leaves shimmered serenely above us glittering with the breeze as we drew ever closer to the enchanting sound. Reaching the far side of the wood we emerged into unbroken sunshine and at once I saw for the first time the fabled waterfalls and the pond into which they ran. The clean-cut chalk from where the water emerged echoed the pristine quality of the young silver birch trees among which we had just walked. Each little stream filled the air with the fresh sounds of babbling water; as the water cascaded over the clean chalk it empowered the pond with a fresh effervescent quality. Some of the streams emerged from horizontal channels cut into the soil above the pond; the water-soaked soil between those channels was home to the most luxuriant of flora.

The silver birch wood and the pond where I saw my first dragonfly. Photograph by Bob Knight 1973.

For a while, I peered into the depths of the clear water to gaze at the shiny fish which darted in vibrant shoals. Then a sight both wonderful and unfamiliar captured my attention for it was the first dragonfly I had ever seen. There were indeed dozens of the radiant blue dragonflies skimming over the surface of the clear water; their striking blue colour caught my eye. As they skipped delicately over the water their fine lucent wings scattered the strong sunlight into a myriad of fine bright colours. To my mind this extraordinary image of dazzling multi-spectral splendour was captivating beyond anything I had hitherto witnessed. The blaze of colour that radiated from those tiny wings seemed to trigger a deep sense of enchantment born of this place that has never since lost its power.

Casting my gaze across the water I became aware of the essence of this hidden land. Far beyond the familiarity of tarmac concrete and brick this was a world apart; it was another world in its own right. Born of the industry of man it was now within the remit of a wholly different force that existed on an altogether different scale of time; with grace and purpose it was of the transcendent. I watched as one of the insects suddenly departed from the others and took to the sky as if caught by a sudden updraught. I watched its ascent as it diminished to a fleck and disappeared into the unblemished blue sky to carry with it a sense of wonder and enlightenment. It was a fleeting but seminal moment in my childhood.

The pond with a little waterfall in the foreground. A winter scene by Bob Knight 1969.

Not far from that pond and close to a railway tunnel was a sight that no child could resist: a locomotive and its dislocated wagons lay silent upon rusting rails. Of course, at that age I expected that all old and abandoned locomotives were steam. I climbed into the locomotive excited at the prospect of something archaic. I was somewhat surprised and a little disappointed to find controls that reminded me of the controls of my father's car. In fact, the ignition switch looked just like that of a motorcar – this was a diesel locomotive.

Funnily enough, at this time when I was around 5 years old our dad frequently took mum and I out for a ride in his car. And as we passed this vast quarry of brilliant white chalk I would gaze down in wonder. My mum used to joke: "Oh! Eric and Clifford have been naughty again. Just look, they took their buckets and spades and dug out that big hole in the ground" Little did our mum know that we brothers were really venturing down into that wonderful dragonfly valley on our surreptitious forays into the realm of long silent diesel locomotives. And luckily through the dedication and the hard work of a group of railway enthusiasts those locomotives would be preserved. An overview of the story of these locomotives and of their preservation is in appendix B.

By the early 1970s two diesel locomotives remained in the third Alpha pit and it was fortunate that the locomotives were removed from the pit for restoration in 1972. The Alpha pits were excavated partly below the water table and up until the early 1970s water was continually pumped from the pits via an electric pump housed in a corrugated iron pump shed close to the western cliff of the third chalk pit. Around the year 1973 pumping was terminated and the chalk pits rapidly began to flood. Very quickly the silver birch woods that had grown in the third chalk pit were submerged apart from the top third of the tree tops. Interestingly, the tree tops continued to produce new leaves in springtime for several years after the wood became flooded. I recall as late as 1978 the curious sight of tree tops sticking out of the lake sporting flourishing new spring leaves.

The third Alpha pit viewed from Buckland Road. Note the railway tunnel at the far end of the quarry. Photograph by Bob Knight 1969.

THE DAWN OF THE TRACK

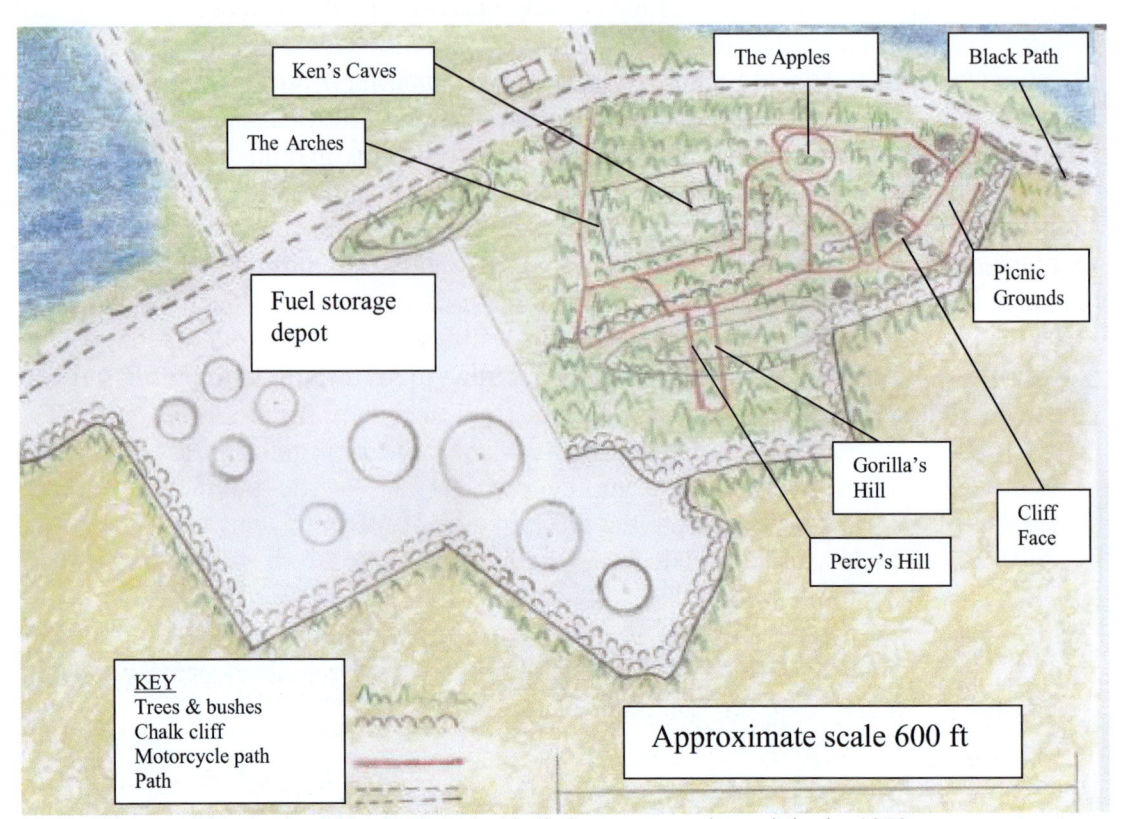

The Track within the Francis Chalk Quarry as we knew it in the 1970s.

While the Alpha pits of Salt Lane were still being excavated, a thick wood had grown in the quiet seclusion of the old Francis Chalk Quarry to the north. Around the year 1962, my cousin Terry Springhall and many of his teenage friends cut the first track for motorbikes among the dense undergrowth of the Francis Chalk Quarry. Thus, the Francis quarry became known to our generation as the Track. Terry Springhall recalls: "John Graves was the chap who came up with the idea of the Track".

Terry had, among other bikes for the Track, a BSA 500cc Gold Star. Terry is the son of Sheila and Perce Springhall, and Terry was also known after his father as "Perce". A hill that lives in the folklore of Cliffe was named after Terry: Percy's Hill. In time, the paths that were cut in the Francis Chalk Quarry from the early 1960s became well trodden and well established. And these paths and hills acquired names born of the affection us locals had for the Track. Percy's Hill was steep and rose to around 30 or 40 feet. Its surface was firm soil and it was a good solid path in that respect. It was wide enough to accommodate a car, and it often did. My brother Victor recalls of the time that Alan Hagger had a Ford Popular from which he removed the windows. In the 1960s an old Ford Popular could be bought from a scrap yard for £10. Alan used to run it up Percy's Hill at such speed that the car would jump over the brow of that hill. Parallel to Percy's was Gorilla's Hill. Gorilla's stood yet higher and ran steeper than Percy's. The surface of Gorilla's was of ever shifting sandy clay; it was a hill only for the seasoned scrambler. Another great challenge was a hill called Cliff Face: it was indeed the face of a small chalk cliff, its angle of slope barely less than 90 degrees in the vertical. The Track was a lively place for many young people in the 1960s and 1970s, young people including Louie Lucock, Ian Pearson and those in the following pictures.

The Track around 1964, photographs courtesy of Terry Springhall.

Terry Springhall with John Smith at Percy's Hill (left)
Ron Taylor, Michael Channon, Roger Hatcher and Terry Springhall at the Picnic Grounds (right)

Terry Springhall at Gorilla's Hill / Terry Sprighall at the Picnic Grounds.

Terry Springhall jumping Percy's Hill / Alan Smith, Roger Hatcher, Terry Springhall and Michael Channon at Percy's Hill.

Alan Smith's "old shed" at Cliff Face in the 1960s. Photograph courtesy of Alan and Donna Smith.

The image that embodies the spirit of the Track: Teri Collins nee Lucock and Louie Lucock in the late 1960s or very early 1970s. Louie was in his element here in the Track. Everyone loved Louie; he was a legend to us. Photograph courtesy of Teri Collins.

THE JET

In 1962, Dick Dowsett was working on the pontoon crane in the Shepherd's Wick Lake. One day he saw some surveyors working along the old tramway adjacent to the lake, and he asked them what was going on. He learned that the surveyors were preparing for the construction of a pipeline in support of a new industry that was coming to Cliffe: a fuel storage depot was to be constructed in part of the Francis Chalk Quarry. Dick was enthusiastic about working there, and indeed he worked at the depot from its opening. Soon the pipeline was laid, and in its construction many of the old railway sleepers of the tramway were dug out to make way for the pipeline's trench[11].

The fuel storage depot brought some significant changes to the Francis Chalk Quarry. Opened under the company Jet on May 13th 1963 the depot operated initially on four fuel storage tanks with more tanks added in later years[11]. To make way for the depot, some of the Victorian era chamber kilns were removed and the face of the chalk hill in which resided the old blacksmiths cave was cut back[1]. A company called William Press performed the groundwork and preparation for the site of the depot[13]. A company called Dick Hampton provided all of the heavy machinery for taking away soil and rubble, and Oxleys constructed the heavy tanks that characterised the depot[13]. Quarry House where the family Parsons lived was within the depot site; although the house was left standing with the building of the depot. The scullery of Quarry House was used as a laboratory during the era of the Francis works[11]. Dick Dowsett remembers that there were old laboratory benches and laboratory paraphernalia in the scullery up until Quarry House was finally demolished in the early 1970s.

Viewed due west, Quarry House at the western end of the Francis Chalk Quarry in the 1950s or early 1960s. This was the home of an old Cliffe family, the Parsons family. Photograph by Albert Smith courtesy of Martyn Smith.

"The Jet", as it was known, was a fuel storage and distribution point for petrol and diesel. Fuel was brought by ship to a quay sited opposite the western side of Cliffe Fort. The fuel was pumped approximately a mile to the depot by way of the buried pipeline which consisted of one large diameter and two smaller diameter pipes. At the depot, lead was added to the petrol to adjust its octane rating[11]. At the depot too, dye and a chemical marker were added to the diesel fuel to meet the requirements of customs[11]. The fuel was distributed by way of road tankers. I recall the depot being known locally as the Jet in the early 1970s and later, as ownership changed, the depot became known locally as the Conoco. The depot closed around the turn of the century and the tanks were removed in the early years of the 21st century.

The fuel storage depot in the mid-1980s. The photograph at the bottom shows the chalk hill upon which once stood the water tank of the old Francis works.
Photographs by Clive Tester.

THE PICNIC GROUNDS

Cliffe Cubs Bob Rayfield, Roy Barton, Clive Morris, Martin Finney, and Lee Smith cooking sausages in the Picnic Grounds in 1973. Photograph courtesy of Adrian Hatcher.

The grassy plateau below the eastern most cliffs of the Francis Chalk Quarry was always known as the Picnic Grounds to us. Back when I was four or five around the end of the 1960s, my sister Kay would oftentimes look after me while my parents worked at the Post Office shop. To the picnic grounds often we would go with our sandwich lunch.

There exists among the people of Cliffe a sense of shared ownership towards Under the Hill. The Picnic Grounds were recognised back in the 1960s and 1970s as a communal place for our village. My friends and I attended the Cliffe cubs in the early 1970s; Alan and Molly Hatcher took us Under the Hill to teach us how to cook in the open. In the Picnic Grounds we learned how to cook sausages on a wood fire. Each sausage was wrapped in aluminium foil and suspended over the fire from a stick. Those were great days in the cubs. Alan and Molly Hatcher always encouraged us in everything that we did; they always had a motivating word for us. Alan and Molly took over the running of Cliffe Cubs from Mr Oakey in the 1960s and continued to run the cubs into the 1980s.

The Picnic Grounds provided a venue for the famous Tester barbeques. These were annual events of the early to mid-1970s organised by my father. The barbeques took place either at the Picnic Grounds or on the grassy area between Cliffe Creek and the Flamingo Lake. I remember one such barbeque at the Picnic Grounds around 1975. My father made a number of lanterns fashioned from coloured plastic in which night light candles shone in warm tones of red and orange. The lanterns were hung on trees all the length of Black Path leading the way into the Picnic Grounds where a large coal fuelled barbeque was prepared. By night fall a large group of extended family and friends of the family had gathered eating kebabs on skewers as long as your arm. There was plenty of wine available. One guest went to a hedge for a call of nature only to disappear down a steep bank that was hidden by dense undergrowth: he needed to be rescued.

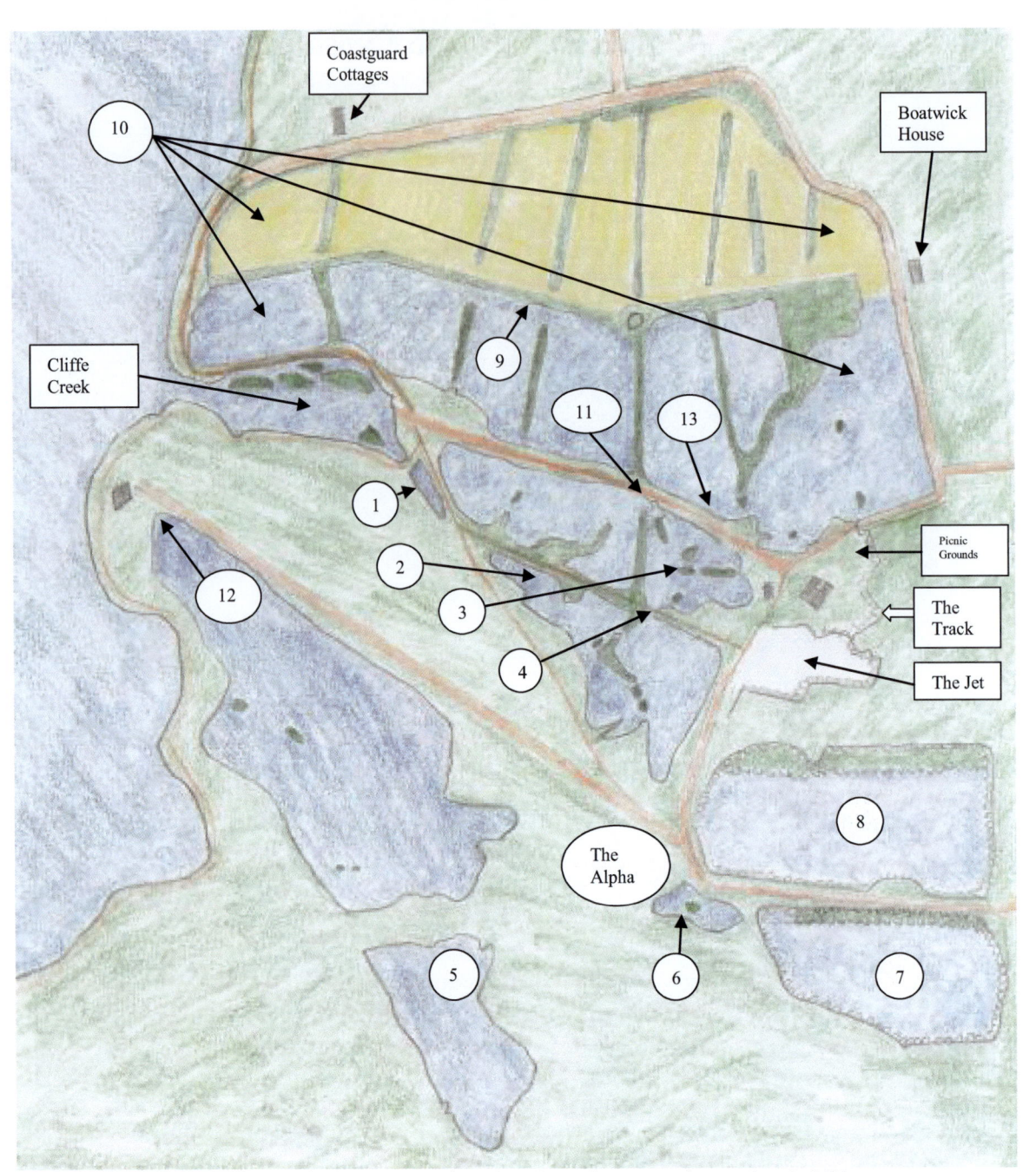

Under the Hill as we knew it in the 1970s. Notations 1 to 5 are the names that we local children gave to the lakes in that time.

Key:-
1: The Flatty
2: The Crystal
3: Swan Lake
4: The Pipes
5: The Sands
6: Second Alpha chalk pit
7: Third Alpha chalk pit
8: Fourth Alpha chalk pit
9: Area where flamingos resided in the early to mid 1970s
10: The lakes to the north and east of Creek Road were known collectively as the Pontoons.
The northern most of the Pontoon lakes were in-filled with river dredgings by the 1970s (shaded yellow).
11: Wellcome yacht club.
12: Blue Circle yacht club
13: Water ski club.

193 CHURCH STREET AND THE FAMILY BUSINESS

Up to 1968, Cliffe Post Office had been run by Mr and Mrs Nunney who operated it from their Chemist shop situated at number 165 Church Street. In August 1968, my parents took over the management of Cliffe Post Office operating it from the premises that our family were already using to manufacture car badges at 193 Church Street. (After the transferral of the Post Office from the Chemist shop, the Chemist at 165 Church Street continued to operate until the 1970s).

My mother had primary responsibility for running the post office. My father ran the car badge business with the help of my mother and my brothers Victor and Eric while my sisters Stella and Kay and brother Clifford helped to look after of me. My mother recalls, after a day's work at the post office, spending long evening hours helping to paint hundreds of car badges at the shop. Close and meticulous work was required to paint the fine details of the badges which were then left in neat rows to dry on a long bench at the workshop. At the shop we had a guard dog called Daisy and a cat called Willum; they were two of the most placid pets you'd ever meet. Willum was an old ginger tom, and when Willum had the urge to sleep, which was quite often, he would stretch out on any space convenient to him. One time my father saw Willum walking across the workshop sporting half a dozen car badges stuck to his fur.

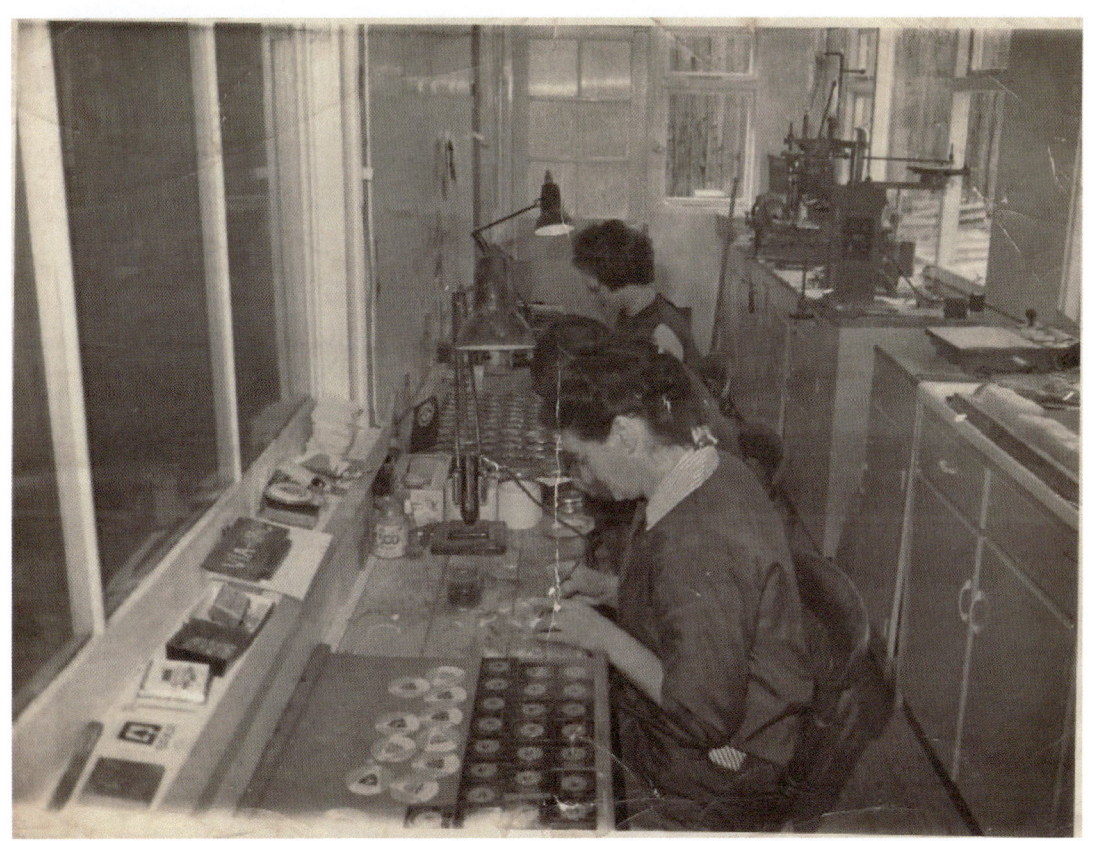

Skilful work. Painting car badges at 193 Church Street in the 1960s: Gwen Tester, Eric Tester and Jill Martin.

My father recalled of working at 193 Church Street in the 1960s and 1970s, for breakfast thick cuts of bacon would be purchased from Parker's. On request, these were sliced at the thickest setting on Parker's meat-cutting machine. Back in the workshop, the rashers were grilled before the red-hot bars of an electric fire.

In the 1960s the bakery across the road from the post office shop was still in operation. My father and brother Victor recalled that in the early morning hours the baker Horace Martin could often be heard beginning work in the bakery with the sound of the dough mixing machine churning away before daybreak. My mother recalls that the bakery had been run by Mr Page and Mr Martin; later Mr Page left the business to emigrate to Australia. My mother recalls that up to the 1960s, the bakery had a small shop selling bread and cakes.

193 Church Street, photograph by Eric Tester 1978. Our neighbours to the left were Jack and Dolly Gales and Jack's brother Sid. To the right lived Dick Ward, former landlord of the Six Bells pub.

It is said locally that 193 Church Street was constructed sometime between the first and second world wars[32]. Former owner of the premises Ernie Bentley told my father that the roof was constructed from wood procured from the Curtis's and Harvey munitions works at Lower Hope Point[32]. In my mother's childhood of the 1930s, the premises were a bicycle shop run by the Bentley family. My mother recalls of the 1930s that the shop sold toys and that there were lots of celluloid dollies displayed in its windows. At this time Mr Ernie Bentley Senior and Mrs Bentley ran the shop with Mrs Bentley serving. Later Ernie Bentley junior took over the business. Ernie junior's son John would later run the garage and petrol station at Church Street. The Tester family in partnership with Roy Hatcher bought 193 Church Street in the early 1960s and set up the car badge manufacturing business under the company registration name *Tester Hatcher*. They purchased the premises from Ella Pennell's uncle Jim Roberts.

Later in the 1960s the business came under the sole ownership of the Tester family. The family business gave employment to some local family friends too: Jill Martin, Marline Mussellwhite, Kath Green and June Harrison worked in the badge business in the 1960s, and Lilly Davis helped to run the post office during the late 1960s and early 1970s. The 1970s was a busy time for the family: in addition to the badge business, my father and brothers Eric and Victor were also rebuilding the adjacent 195 Church Street which was completed in 1977.

The badge making business came to an end in 1977, and the associated machinery of the business was sold. From 1980 to 1982, 193 Church Street was almost completely rebuilt with its corrugated iron and wood being replaced with brick concrete and red roof tiles. During this period the post office was temporally relocated to an annex of 195 Church Street. It was now my turn to work in the business and I helped my father with this project in evenings after school, at weekends, and through the school holidays. Uncle Perce and Hoo man Ken Mundy and son helped with the demolition and building work along with brother Eric between his new job at Kingsnorth Power Station and Steve Holroyd too. I recall, during the rebuilding work, breaking up the heavy concrete blocks on which once stood the badge pressing machines on which my brothers Victor and Eric had worked late into the nights and 7 days a week back in the days of the badge business. I recall pulling down the old wooden panelled partition wall between the badge making workshop and the post office. I found, on a cross beam behind the wall, an empty match box next to which was an unsmoked cigar. It was a small cigar of the type with a tapered end. My father surmised that back in the early part of the century the builder of the wall had run out of matches, left his cigar on a convenient ledge, and had then inadvertently boarded it up.

Jill Martin and my parents and I ran the grocery store at n° 193 in the period 1982 to 1984. I recall serving many of the familiar names of the village in our shop: To name but a few, Harold and Jessie Weavers, Violet and Perce Channon, Daisy and Graham Hoggarth, Ray Francis, Robert Ambrose, Roy Harrison, Les and Dorothy Harrison. Les Harrison was the brother of Roy, and like Roy and all the Harrison brothers Les shared an appreciation of our marshes. I remember Les and Dorothy as a nice and friendly couple who would always find the time to exchange pleasantries. I would frequently meet Les and Dorothy enjoying a walk Under the Hill.

Sadly, Jill Martin passed away unexpectedly in 1984, and at this point the grocery store was discontinued. My mother would continue to run the post office at 193 Church Street. I remember my mother worked at lightning speed processing the post office transactions with efficiency and accuracy. Every Friday evening my mother would total up the transactions for the week in the Balance Book, and check this against the cash remaining in the post office. The balance was always correct. On mum's retirement in 1993, the post office auditors came out to Cliffe Post Office to do a final check. On parting they told my mum that they always enjoyed coming out to Cliffe to audit as they knew that under my mum's management everything would always be in good order. Mum had many well wishes from the people of Cliffe. Daisy Hoggarth put together a "This is your life" album for mum's retirement; it was beautifully illustrated with Daisy's own cartoons.

From 1993 until 2004 the post office was run from the premises by a number of stand-in managers. The building was sold and subsequently demolished in 2005.

Mum at the Post Office in 1985 with the Balance Book on her right.

THE MOON AND THE MORNING STAR

1968 is a time that stands out in my mind because in order for my mum to run the post office I went to a child minder, Mrs Corrall, just across the road from the shop at Longford House. Mrs Corrall had a son Adam who was my age, and I have good memories of my days at Mrs Corrall's house. The house to me seemed wonderfully mysterious. Downstairs there was a small door that led to the cellar, and in one of the bedrooms where Adam and I played was a little door that must have led to the attic: I was always filled with a sense of intrigue about these curious little doors and to what places they might lead. Sometimes my mum would appear at the post office window and Mrs Corrall would call me so that we could wave. When the shop closed for the day my mum would be doing paper work at the post office and I would sometimes spend early evening running around the chequered lino floor of the shop. The post office shop also sold cards, and later accommodated a pharmacy. The photograph below was taken at the post office at Christmas 1968. Each Christmas, workers at the Alpha received a bonus in the form of gift tokens. My mother had to order these in especially; it was a big event for a small village post office. The two gentlemen in the photograph were from the management of the cement works and my mother is handing over the £5 gift tokens to them.

Cliffe Post Office Christmas 1968. My mother Gwen Tester handing over the Christmas bonus gift vouchers to Cliffe cement works managers. Photograph courtesy of Gwen Tester.

The late 1960s was an interesting time to be a young child, and one aspect of that time had a big influence on me. I recall one time watching television at Longford House with Mrs Corrall's son Adam. It was a special TV program showing live images from a Moon flight. I remember Mrs Corrall's daughters Sue and Tina, who were secondary school age, telling me that the astronauts are flying around the Moon but not landing on it. That would place this particular memory in either December 1968 for Apollo 8 or May 1969 for Apollo 10. These two flights were precursor missions to the Moon prior to the first landing. Of course, at the age of three I had no understanding of the concept of developmental test flights. I remember thinking: why did they go all the way to the Moon and not land? There was an air of expectancy at that time: an anticipation of the day soon to come when man would walk on the Moon.

For bedtime story, my mother read to me a book on how the Moon landings were accomplished. It was a children's book which explained all of the major aspects of a Moon flight; I got a good grasp on the concepts involved. I was particularly fascinated with the fiery hot re-entry into our planet's atmosphere when the Apollo space capsule was returning to earth. As my mother explained, the intense heat experienced on the outside of the space capsule was due to the high speed at which the spacecraft was travelling as it came back into earth's atmosphere. I thought to myself what a wondrous thing this was to be travelling so fast that such heat is created. As a young child I really picked up on that sense of wonder. The talk in our family home at 5 Rookery Crescent was often of the Moon flights that were taking place in the late 1960s and early 70s. I got a good grasp of what was going on from the conversations of my parents, elder brothers and sisters. I remember in January 1971 at the time of the Apollo14 Moon flight that snow had fallen overnight. Maybe only a centimetre had fallen and I was out in Swingate Avenue trying to gather enough snow to make a big bounder size snowball that I could roll round to Rookery Crescent. Eric came looking for me to say that preparations were being televised for the Apollo 14 launch that day and I should come in and see it. And like all of the Moon flights, we followed it from launch to splashdown while sitting in front of the living room Rayburn radiantly hot with coal delivered to our coal shed by the coal man Ted Hodson. There was something very positive and inspirational about the big engineering that got us to the Moon. The missions from 1968 to 1972, presented by James Burke and Patrick Moore, were covered superbly on the television. The Moon landings influenced me and many young people of our generation to follow technical careers in adulthood.

Back in 1968 I attended the nursery at the Co-Op at Church Street (later re named the Universal Stores). There I would see some faces who would become familiar to me as we grew up in Cliffe: among them Paul Enticknap, Alec Pennell, Adrian Hatcher, Lynn McColley, Lorna Hammond, Sarah Hunt, John Rodford and Helen Ebbs. Mrs McColley ran the nursery and it was situated on the top floor of the Co-Op the entrance to the stairs of which was at the northern end of the building. I remember to this day the smell that always greeted me as I climbed the stairs leading to the nursery; it was redolent of bread dough. During this period too, films were sometimes shown in the upstairs room of the Co-Op which my brother Clifford took me to see.

The Co-Op, later to be renamed the Universal Stores at Church Street Cliffe. The front of the shop is boarded off in preparation for its demolition. Photograph by Clive Tester July 1985.

Sometime in 1969 or 1970, the nursery moved to the newly opened Cliffe Memorial Hall. Many years before, a village fund had been started to build the hall to which my grandparents and many others in the village contributed[3]. In September 1970, we came of the age to start school proper. With Alec Pennell, Adrian Hatcher, Stephen Knight, Lorna Hammond, Nicola Green, Linda Smith, Sarah Hunt, Wendy Silver,

Joanne Hearson, Mark Long, David Read, Trevor Joslin, Helen Ebbs, Paul Enticknap, Tracy Milton, Dawn Arthur, Haley Watkins, Neil Thomas and others. In the years below us were Bryan Mooney, Chris Parnell, Martin Hearson, Alan Bush, Mark Godden, Trevor Beagley, Lesly Enticknap, Jane Millington, Sally-Ann Green, Tina Tyres. In the years above us were Edwin Smith, Gary Joslin, John Wassell, Lee Smith, Clive Darker, Colin Darker, Graham Bush, Neil Flook, Neil Henry, Robert Rayfield, Paul Godden, Lyn and Alan Enticknap, Keith Beagley, Philip Cowling, David Milton, Robert Bush and Janice Dowsett. We will always remember Edwin Smith as a lively and energetic lad, a friend who would be taken from us in a tragic accident so young. Likewise, we remember Gary Joslin, another friend who was taken from us so tragically young, and our friend Graham Bush taken from us sadly in his teenage years.

We started school at the infant's school at Norwood Corner. Our first teacher was Mrs Rose, and in our classroom a coal fire blazed away in the winter months. Mid-morning, we would have our milk. Milk was delivered in small milk bottles from Mr Filmer's dairy bearing the name Filmer & Son Courtsole Farm Cliffe in red lettering. In the winter, the milk was left to warm behind the big wire fireguard of the coal fire.

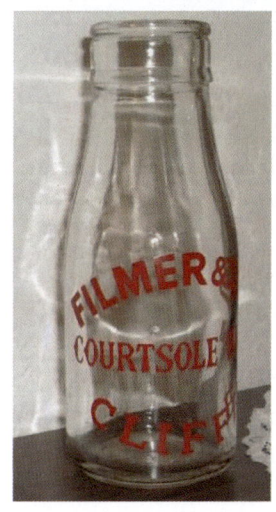

Infant school milk bottle of Cliffe, courtesy of Don and Ross Pople.

School presented a new routine, and the early morning starts afforded an opportunity for an exciting new discovery for me. I recall mum getting me ready for school on a dark winter morning and we could see a brilliant star blazing in the twilight sky to the east just above Ron and Joy Hatcher's house: it was the Morning Star, the planet Venus.

Derek and Kath Green took us to school in the mornings and collected us from school in the afternoons in their dormobile. I always sat next to Alec Pennell on the dormobile, and at school too. Alec's mum and my mum were good school friends; Alec and I had a lot in common. Alec would be a good friend to me all through our schooling. Skilled and resourceful he was a great buddy during our camping trips Under the Hill later in our teenage years.

Alec and I lived opposite to each other at Rookery Crescent, and Derek would always stop the dormobile half way between our two houses to let us off after school. Alec and I had a little competitive game when the Moon landings were taking place in the early 1970s: when Derek dropped us off, Alec and I would run as quickly as we could to our respective houses. We would compare mental notes the next day at school to see who had got the television on first and who had seen first the progress of that day on the Moon. When we talk about manned space flight today in 2015, it is to the International Space Station (ISS): a shining beacon in our night sky that speaks of cooperation between nations; it is a great political achievement of the post Cold War era. The ISS orbits somewhere in the order 200 miles altitude, which is about as far from the earth as any man or woman has ventured since the final Moon landing in 1972. The Moon's orbit lies a thousand times further away from the earth than does the orbit of the ISS. And the prospect of a manned Moon landing taking place within the lifetime of anyone over the age of 40 today has in a real sense receded back into the realm of science fiction. Just imagine from the perspective of today, Alec Pennell and I drinking milk that was sourced from the cows of Cliffe Marshes and warmed before the coal fire of a school that has been rubble now for over 30 years and talking about what man was doing on the Moon that week. That was a special era indeed in which we lived as children; looking back it still amazes me today.

Around 1972, the school at Norwood Corner closed as the new Cliffe primary school opened. The new school had something great for us children - a swimming pool. At the new primary school, I would meet David Arnold and Terry and Danny Kybett. In the summer holidays of the early 1970s David and I would spend the days swimming in the pool. One of our teachers Mrs Barker and her son supervised the swimming pool during the summer holidays. We had great times and we thank them.

Rookery Crescent had been built in 1950, and the houses and gardens were spacious compared to the Victorian era terrace houses that working class families like ours had known. The years following the war had been austere for our parent's generation. In the early years of my parent's marriage in the 1950s, mum worked day shifts at the Uralite in Higham, and my father worked night shifts at Elliot's in Rochester. My father would cycle to Rochester to start the late shift, and en-route wave to my mother coming home on the bus from the early shift. At harvest time in the 1950s, my mother would earn extra money fruit picking after her early shift at the Uralite.

My childhood memories of Rookery Crescent in the early 1970s was of a gardener's pride. Adjoining our house was Ted and Peg Frost at number 7. Ted kept a magnificently colourful front garden. As a young child I would marvel at the viola and antirrhinum flowering just over the low red brick garden wall; Ted's garden was a multitude of scent and colour. Likewise, John and Lilly Davis next to Ted and Peg Frost kept a wonderfully colourful front garden. Joy and Ron Hatcher on our other side always kept an immaculate vegetable garden with a rhubarb patch big enough for me to hide in.

On Saturday mornings, Jack Parker would bring through our back door a huge box of groceries. Jack Parker was a gentleman; he would always address me as Sir when I came into his shop to buy fruit or sweets. On Wednesdays Harold Loveland would come around the village in his Co-Op bread van. It was the "bun round" as we called it. Mum would buy buns and bitter lemon. If Alec and I were playing in Rookery Crescent, we would always talk with Harold. Placid and gentle, Harold would let us sit among the sweet smelling fresh bread on the back of his van as he drove up Rookery Crescent at a speed a bit slower than walking pace. When he stopped for his next call, he would give us both a boiled sweet.

This was the time before main drainage came to Cliffe. The houses that comprised Thatcher's Lane, Rookery Crescent, Swingate Avenue Wadlands Road and Quickrells Avenue were known colloquially at that time as the New Estate. And a feature of the New Estate that set it apart from the older roads of Cliffe was a centralised sewage system which meant that that each house did not require its own cesspit. The drainage from the New Estate was channelled collectively to a sewage treatment plant located at the southern end of Thatcher's Lane. Us children called it the Sand Pit (pronounced Sampit), as there were always piles of sand around that sewage plant. Behind the tall wire fence of the Sampit was a curious structure comprising of a concave wall built of the same red brick as Rookery Crescent and spouting from its side a peculiarly oversized faucet. The Sampit's main features were square concrete lined sewage ponds from which regularly emanated strange gushing and gurgling sounds. The ponds were emptied periodically: a lorry with a large cylindrical tank would arrive, and the sludge would be pumped into the tank to be taken away. The disturbance of the sludge normally caused a pungent stench to drift throughout the New Estate – the lorry became known locally as the Lavender Lorry[3]. Main drainage came to Cliffe around 1972, and soon after Rookery Lodge was built over the redundant Sampit.

Our house, 5 Rookery Crescent in the early 1970s. The brick shed was full of motorcycle parts for re-building motorbikes for Under the Hill. With the Track on our doorstep, many a shed of Cliffe would be given over to teenage motorbike mechanics to hone their skills. The motorcycle in the photograph is my brother Eric's 350 cc Matchless. Photograph by Eric Tester.

CLIFFE SHOPS OF THE EARLY 1970s

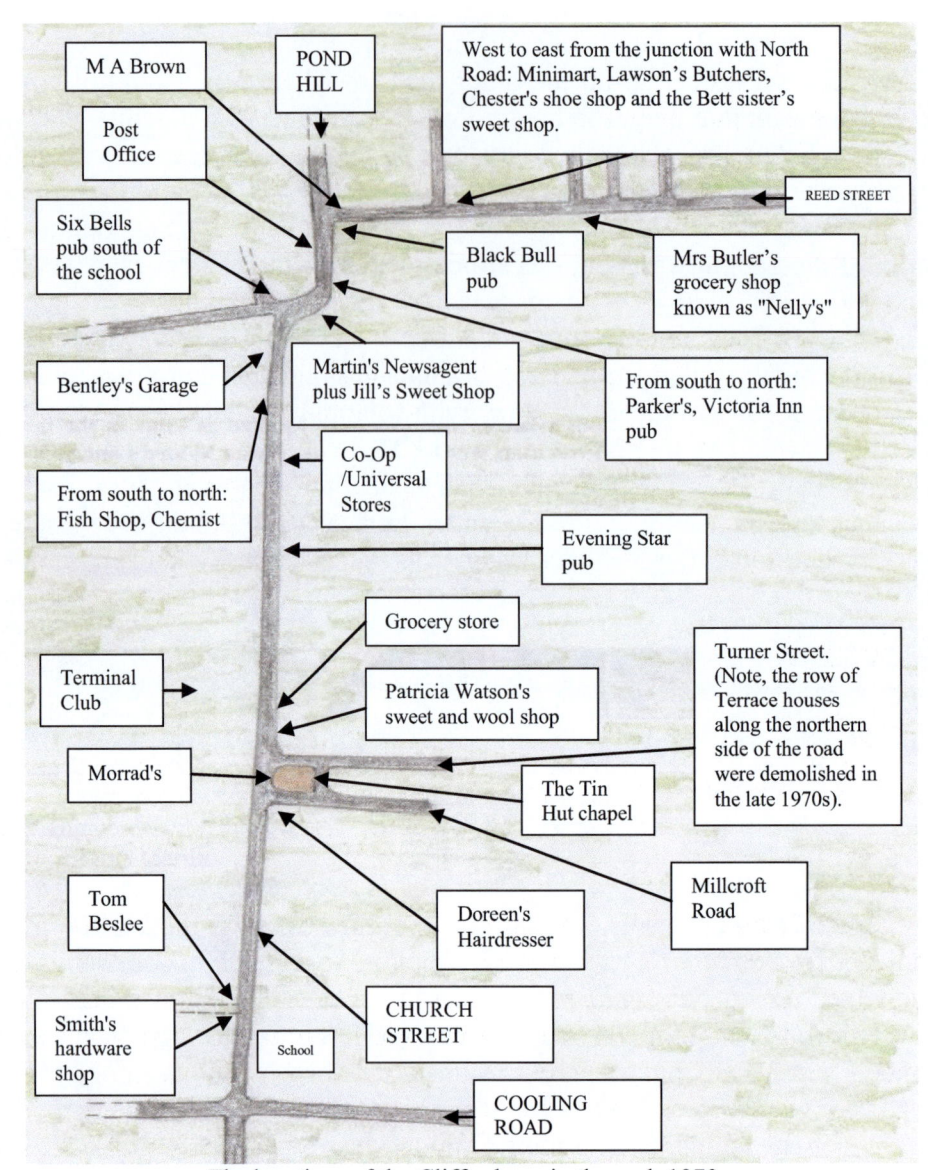

The locations of the Cliffe shops in the early 1970s.

Mr and Mrs Smith ran a hardware shop at the house that was formerly Polly Ward's shop at number 41 Church Street. From Mr and Mrs Smith's I remember as a teenager buying blakeys for my boots: I recall always a friendly welcome from Mr and Mrs Smith.

Morrad's shop closed sometime during the 1970s, and around the end of the 1970s the row of houses in which Morrad's resided was demolished to make way for the new surgery. Up to this time, Cliffe surgery was held at the Red House in Reed Street.

The school next to Cliffe Church closed around 1972 following the opening of the new school at Church Street. Use of the old school buildings continued as the venue for Cliffe Cubs and also for the Scene Seventy youth club. The youth club was run over the years from the 1960s onward by many volunteers who gave of their time to provide this excellent club for the village youth. Among them, the Vicar Mr Smith, Marie Vyse, Ross Walkinshaw, Jessie Weavers, Grenville Bush, Mr Jeffrey and more.

For four years during the 1960s, June Bailey, Lynn Bowdrey, Mick Bowdrey and Ian Pearson ran a church youth club in the old Butchers shop at Church Street opposite the Victoria Inn. The premises were owned by the church and given to them free. June, Lynn, Mick and Ian also ran a junior club called "size 11" for children up to 11 years of age above the Co-Op grocers at Church Street[37].

Another well-known institution dating from before the 1970s and operating into the present day is the Temperance Club situated on Church Street near to the junction with Swingate Avenue. Originally a Methodist Church, it served as an infant's school for some years after 1902[25A]. Stan Beeching recalls that in 1936 or 1937 the building came under the remit of the Alpha who set up a games club in the building for its workers. Stan recalls that he helped to install the billiard table in 1936/37; heavy lead slabs were used in the construction of the table.
In later years Len Batchelor Senior and Junior of Warf Farm bought the premises in order to save the building from demolition[3], and from where the Snooker Club continued with many members including Len Batchelor Sr and Jr, Whack Knight, Bill Smith, Steve and David Martin. This photograph was taken in recent times by Clive Tester.

Up until the mid-1970s Miss Brown, who had taken on the running of the shop from her parents in the 1940s, continued to run the sweet shop at the junction of Reed Street/Church Street. Wendy Meader nee Henderson recalls that in 1978 the shop was sold to her parents Fred and Pat Henderson of the Victoria Inn, and the sweet shop was opened as Pat's Shop. At this time Wendy and Tony Meader took over the running of the Victoria Inn.

A shop that all of us children liked to visit was the Bett sister's sweet shop at Reed Street. The sisters had taken the shop over from their parents upon their retirement. Walking into the shop we were greeted by a wonderful smell of sweets, matched by the sister's kind and cordial nature: they loved us coming into their shop.

An institution of the time was Martin's paper shop opposite the Six Bells. Martin's sold everything from bicycle parts and Wellington boots to pink paraffin. Like the other shops in Cliffe, a warm subtle aroma of paraffin greeted customers in the winter months; some twenty years before the introduction of gas to Cliffe, the shops and some of the houses in Cliffe were heated with paraffin heaters. And Martin's was where my brothers and I and most of Cliffe folk had their haircut. Fred Martin had a unique methodology to his hair cutting. With a touch of his hand, he would manoeuvre the head into all sorts of precise angles to facilitate his job. Martin's shop was a lively friendly and busy family business; in the early 1970s I remember family members Tom, Fred, Peg, Reg, Geoff and Pam all working in the shop. Jill Martin ran a sweet shop at the western end of the premises. Jill was always great with us children and enjoyed us coming into the shop. If we bought a carton of orange juice, Jill would always look down the straw to make sure that no beetles were hiding in that straw – I think Jill had once had an unpleasant experience with a beetle in a straw. My family knew Jill Martin as Aunt Jill; Jill was a close family friend. I remember Jill spending Christmases with us in the early 1970s and making jigsaw puzzles with us children. One Easter I recall, Aunt Jill bought me a Pink Panther Easter egg.

"Aunt Jill". Jill Martin 1930 - 1984.

A little way from Martin's was John Bentley's petrol station; it was built of green painted wood. It is said in the village that the petrol station was constructed from wood procured from the Curtis's and Harvey munitions works at Lower Hope Point. The old building of the petrol station was pulled down and replaced around the year 1975. From Bentley's petrol station, fuel for another institution of Cliffe would have been procured – petrol for motorcycling Under the Hill.

Another structure in Cliffe that originated from the Curtis's and Harvey munitions works is this green corrugated iron barn just to the east of Morning Cross at Cooling Road[11]. Like Bentley's garage, the original paintwork is a distinctive green colour. John Mark Tester is in this photograph, and one hundred years before, John's great grandfather Ernest Burton worked at the munitions works from where this barn originated. Photograph by Frila Tester July 2015.

FREE AS A BANTAM

Motorcycling Under the Hill was an integral part of the youth culture of our village. It was but one expression of the special freedom that Under the Hill gave to us. From the stony potholed road at the bottom of Pond Hill to Cliffe Fort and beyond was a special place for the young of Cliffe. In the 1960s my sister Stella bought a green 125cc BSA bantam for £5 from Cliffe man Mr Holly. Stella used to ride the Bantam Under the Hill, and once met the challenge of Percy's Hill. At this time too, Cliffe Creek was a popular venue for leisure and swimming for my sister Stella and fiancé Steve Holroyd, my sister Kay and fiancé Dave Green, James Godden, John Ashby, Ian Pearson, Andy and Janet Keats, Barry Ashby and many others. At the end of the 1960s, Stella passed the Bantam on to sister Kay. To my eye the Bantam was aesthetically pleasing in form with its stylish teardrop petrol tank. My brother Eric had a succession of motorbikes for Under the Hill. He had a couple of AJS machines: a Matchless 350 made in 1950 and a Matchless 500 made in 1955. The year of manufacture of these machines was stamped on the engine case. The Matchless' that Eric owned were built at the AJS works in Dartford. Eric also had a Bantam 125, a Villiers 200 and a Norton Jubilee. Eric and brother in law Steve Holroyd built a bike out of Norton frame and a Villiers 225cc engine. Eric coined a phrase for this hybrid: Norton-Villiers. Up Rookery Crescent those bikes would be pushed all the way to the bottom of Pond Hill where the realm of Under the Hill began. Pillion I would ride on Kay or Eric's motorbikes. Sometimes we would go to the sea wall at lower Hope Point. I can still picture that journey as I saw it, riding on the petrol tank and looking out from an oversized half face crash helmet. At this time the most northerly of the pontoon lakes were still water filled and constituted a broad expanse of water from Boatwick House all the way beyond the Coastguard Cottages. As we rode past the Coastguard Cottages I remember a pair of long ores hanging on the southern wall of the terrace.

We could ride far and wide around the sea wall of our village, but the Track was the true realm of the motorbikes. It was the place where the freedom enjoyed by the youth of Cliffe often found its greatest expression. On any given weekend or holiday, a group of Cliffe youths would be found along the paths cut amid the deep brambles of the old Francis Chalk Quarry taking the challenge of its hills on pushbikes or on motorbikes like the elegant little Bantam. And to this day, when I catch the sweet oily aroma of a 2-stroke engine it takes me back to the end of the 1960s to be a small child there deep within the wonderful labyrinth of mysterious hidden paths in a place that we all once knew as the Track. It was a time of stylish old British bikes of long faded colours patched up and resurrected for their new purpose. A time when modified exhaust pipes pulsed with sharp ear ringing energy that was felt as much as heard. A time of improvisation, of bare HT leads wrapped around spark plugs that threatened a powerful jolt should you dare to put your hand too near. A time when bikes with leaky acid batteries fell before those fabled hills to cause the chalky soil of the Track of bubble and fizz. A time when the cliffs that encompassed our Track towered above us like mountains, and the lakes that lay beyond were vast and unknowable places of boundless depth. A time when it seemed that this wild unrestricted and untamed land we called Under the Hill was given to all children.

The wonderful labyrinth of mysterious hidden paths in a place that we all once knew as the Track. The silos and chimneys of the cement works at Salt Lane, then in its final year of operation, lie beyond the huge white tanks of the Jet. Quarry House is on the upper mid-right. A concrete wall and arch of the Francis Chamber Kiln of the Victorian era is at the upper far right. Photograph by Bob Knight 1969.

Left: Circa 1966, Ian Pearson on his Royal Enfield 500 cc Bullet with Robert Saunders in the sidecar. The sidecar was a bits-n-pieces Watsonian with a "small wheel conversion" by Ian's Dad Louis (Cliff or Cliffy) Pearson. In the background is a petrol road tanker of the newly constructed petrol storage depot, and behind that can be seen the roof and chimney of Quarry House. Photograph courtesy of Ian Pearson.

Below: Eric's 350cc Matchless ridden by my father at Cliff Face in the Track in 1974. Photograph by Eric Tester.

The Track in the snow circa 1970: Sliding at speed down Percy's Hill children play on an improvised sledge made from a car roof. Photographs by Herbert Weber.

My mother and my aunt Daphne enjoy a picnic with their children in the Picnic Grounds in the 1950s.

It was through an isthmus between the lakes of Under the Hill, Creek Road, on which we walked on days when the motorbikes were left at home. By the time I was four or five, Creek Road had become an integral part of my world. We would walk that way in the summer months when the flints that made up the length of Creek Road glinted in the sun. That old flint road always seemed to shimmer with a warm orangey aura in summer. We would go that way in winter weekends too: my brothers Eric and Clifford once made a vow that they would swim at the Creek once a week for an entire year – And they did, and after the brief cold winter swim warmed themselves before a driftwood fire lit on the banks of the Creek.

The old flint road to the creek.

Creek Road was an active place at that time. A water skiing club was established in the Bundy Lake by the 1970s; they had built a wooden quay with a good concrete base. And half way along Creek Road stood the Wellcome Yacht Club with a long row of yachts parked upon the bank of the "Opposite Joes Lake". It was a place that became familiar to my young and acute ears: the tall hollow masts and fine tackle lines whistled and tapped out a simple melodic mantra in the wind as we walked past. It was the wind's free song, easy and uncomplicated, so much a part of the ambiance of Under the Hill.

Near to the yacht club is a break in the tree line that allows one to look due south and to the direction of the Alpha. I remember when we reached this point I would look due south to see a pontoon crane in operation. From a distance of around 500 metres the tall arm of the crane seemed reassuringly graceful in its movement. The image of the crane reflected a sense of purposefulness, tall among the flatlands, bowing obligingly in its motion. Then one weekend I looked and the crane was in movement no more. This would have marked the closure of the Alpha in April 1970. My uncle Sid had a memory as a young boy in the mid 1920s of chalk being dug from the Francis Chalk Quarry and sent up by locomotive to the whiting works at the Creek. Sid had witnessed the closing years of an industrial infrastructure that had its roots in the Victorian era. Fifty year later, I was witnessing the last days of what had been known in Sid's youth as the new factory.

Nearing the Creek on the northern side of the road was one of the remaining relics of the Victorian cement works. It was a vast concrete building with its flat roof supported by many concrete columns. Many thought that it was reminiscent in form to the buildings of classical Greek architecture. The building was later demolished, as Adrian Hatcher and I recall, around the year 1976. In the photograph of Molly and Alan Hatcher at Creek Road in chapter 2, that building can be seen on the right of the photograph. The building was known locally as Caller's Ruins as recalled by Bob Knight.

Caller's Ruins near Cliffe Creek. Photograph by Bob Knight 1969.

There was magic to the creek of my early childhood: it had its own life and character that was personified in a salty aroma to the creek air. The smell of the creek had the allure of seaweed and rocks and the curiosities that lie beneath. On still summer days, the tide might rise without a wave ebbing gently up the creek's concrete walls and sluices. The silently ebbing power of the tide intrigued me as it filled our vast creek leaving in its wake puddles in the salt marsh where little crabs hid. And at low tide, a swim could still be had in the tidal water that was retained in the fleet to the south of the creek. We knew this little fleet as the Flatty. Our long days at the creek would bring to me a sound that became so familiar to my ears as to be synonymous with Under the Hill: the distant ring of the bell buoy. Like the foghorn's far-away howl on foggy days, its distant tone seemed to draw my imagination deeper into the wild lands of Under the Hill.

The view due east from the top of Caller's Ruins. The Wellcome yacht club building can be seen at Creek Road. Photograph by Bob Knight 1969.

It was at Cliffe Creek that we met Herbert Weber who would come to play an important part in our childhood days. Herbert was from Germany and had been a prisoner of war in World War Two. He had settled in England after the Second World War. I remember a time came when I was around 5 years of age and I decided that it was time for me to swim in the creek along with my older brothers. But it was of course too early for me to swim in the creek and my siblings were having none of it. I made some noisy tearful protests, which Herbert placated by taking me upon his shoulders and wading through the shallow creek water to an island that lays five or so metres from the bank. He sat me on the island for a few minutes and I was happy. On return he produced for me some sweets from his bicycle saddlebag.

Herbert with my brother Eric on the left during a cycling holiday in North Wales in the early 1970s. Herbert, in his denim jeans and denim jacket with his bicycle, was a familiar figure on Cliffe Marshes from the 1960s to the 1980s.

Cliffe Creek circa 1971. Herbert and my brothers built this raft from driftwood. The boys on the raft are my brothers Clifford and Eric Tester. The girl sitting on the sea wall is my sister Kay. The boy in the red jumper with the Fred Martin haircut is me. The man behind the camera was Herbert Weber.

An addition to Cliffe Creek that would become part of the creek's character came around 1972. A young couple, an Englishman and his Spanish wife, were sailing a modest size wooden boat on the Thames[32]; the boat was called Moonlit Waters. The boat started to take on water and the couple sailed it into Cliffe Creek and secured it to the concrete Warf at the eastern end of the creek[32]. There it resided listing heavily. The couple decided to abandon the boat and return home[32]. Herbert helped them to salvage some of their belongings from its waterlogged hull[32]. By some agreement the boat came under the ownership of a Mr Skinner of Pond Hill. Mr Skinner kept the boat moored at the Creek making some repairs and the boat was soon righted. Sometime in the 1970s ownership transferred to a couple who had a young son of toddler age. This family lived at the creek on Moonlit Waters until the boat was moved out of the creek and relocated in Hoo Marina in 1984.

Moonlit Waters at Cliffe Creek circa 1972. Photograph by Herbert Weber.

Moonlit Waters shortly after its arrival at Cliffe Creek. Photograph by Eric Tester circa 1972.

Moonlit Waters was not the first ailing vessel to find a resting place on the shores of Cliffe. The Hans Egede came to Cliffe in 1962 (date reference Allan Cherry: *A Pictorial History of Cooling and Cliffe*). This familiar landmark is shown here with Richard Tester in 2002.

The Hans Egede. Photograph by Clive Tester.

THE HISTORY MAN

A picture of Cliffe Creek and the clay lakes of Cliffe Marshes would not be complete without reference to a man whose presence in that land was as familiar as the elder trees, blackberry thickets and dog rose bushes that still today flourish in the meadowlands between those lakes. When I first met him at the end of the 1960s shortly after he came to the flatlands of the Thames Estuary, his hair was of a man still of youth. By the time of his return to his homeland twenty years later, his hair was the very shade of white of the elder blossom that still today greets summer on the banks of his beloved clay lakes. His name was Max Herbert Weber, known to us all as Herbert.

Herbert was unconventional for a man of his age within that time. His attire was always of faded denim jeans and denim jacket. The only exception to this dress code was when he was at work: Herbert worked as a civilian clerk at the Chattenden Army bomb disposal unit to which he wore collar and tie in smart attire. But it was sun-bleached denim that personified Herbert's real character. Herbert was an eternal youth who felt only truly at home "out in the sticks" as he used to phrase it. His demeanour was echoed too in his bicycle. It was the first bicycle that he purchased. It was a Claude Butler 5 derailleur geared racing bike, and he bought it brand new in 1953. By the time that I knew Herbert, that bike was already twenty years old: the bike's faded and worn paintwork matched well Herbert's own wind and sun weathered features. I have this bicycle today, and one day just as Herbert passed it on to me it will be passed on to my own sons.

What struck many people during their initial conversations with Herbert was the precision with which he spoke. His use of the language, through that strong German accent that I can so clearly recall to this day, spoke of a man of analytical mind and natural linguist talent. But there too in his mannerisms were conveyed his undeniable modesty. He learned to speak English during his mid-20s as a prisoner of war, and he was quick to adopt some quaintly English expressions. If some mishap were to occur, for example if we were out cycling miles from home and his bicycle sprang a flat tire, "Oh Crikey" would be his first words.

Herbert was born on February 17th 1920 in a village near to the city of Leipzig in Germany. His formative years were in the great depression of that time: something that likely shaped part of his character – he was frugal by nature and scrupulously independent. An old story that Herbert used to relate to us of the depression was of the enormous quantities of next to worthless money notes that were in the average wage packet. The story told of a man who took his weekly wage home in a suitcase. The case was stuffed to bulging with the money. On the way home that suitcase was snatched, but not for the money it contained. The money was found abandoned in a pile, the thief lightening the load by dumping the money that was worth far less than the suitcase he wanted. Herbert told me something of his boyhood. His parents owned a smallholding and raised pigs and chickens: a way of life that my mother was familiar with. He and the other children at his school walked in bare feet throughout the summer months; a sign of the times that my father was familiar with too. My father grew up in Chatham in the 1930s, and many of my father's school friends attended school in shoes so worn that their toes were protruding through big holes. My father recalled that sometimes a boy in his class would be given a note by his parents to say that he would not attend school the following day because his shoes were going to be repaired. In fact, Herbert and my parents had much in common being raised in the same austere times. Herbert would remain a good friend to my parents and all my family.

Herbert's father was a trade unionist and experienced a disturbing event when the Nazis came to power in Germany. Suspicious of anything that suggested politics of the left, the Nazis searched the Weber household and confiscated some union related paper work. Thankfully nothing else came of this. Throughout the Second World War, Herbert to his own surprise was never called into the military. He worked in a civilian role as a clerk in the German air force. He was posted to various places around Germany. He recalled some very cold winters with weather so cold that diesel froze in the fuel tanks of lorries, and the trunks of trees made brittle by the cold broke under the weight of the snow that they bore. During the war, news came one day of a failed assassination attempt on Hitler. Herbert recalled that many of his colleagues were quietly voicing regret that the attempt had been unsuccessful: many held the view that the war should be ended, and this might have come about if Hitler had been killed in that assassination attempt.

In 1945 with the allies advancing on Germany, a rifle was finally put into Herbert's hands. He was called back to his hometown for the final standoff. In these last weeks of the war just about all of the German civilians, young and old, were called to arms. He found the person in charge of the group that he was assigned to was his old schoolmaster. There were some young members of the group who were excited at the prospect of fighting. Some of them had the "it won't happen to me" attitude, as Herbert put it. This bravado soon withered when some shots were exchanged and a few members of the group got injured. In fact, Herbert and likely the vast majority of the group were keen to be taken prisoner without further bloodshed. The group retreated into a barn. They became aware of some activity outside of the barn; as they had expected it was the allies. Waiting quietly, Herbert saw the barn door open and the barrel of a machine gun emerge from outside. He hoped that no one in his group would try to "play the hero". If so, a spay of bullets from the machine gun would have ended it all. Luckily no one from his group put up resistance, and they were all taken prisoner by the Americans.

Herbert and his fellow prisoners of war were taken across the Atlantic in a convoy of ships which moved at the speed of the slowest ship in that convoy. It was a long sea crossing during which some of the prisoners suffered terrible seasickness. Some could not eat during that long voyage, and at the end of the journey, emaciated, needed to be carried off of the ship on stretchers. Though Herbert suffered no seasickness. The ship sailed up the Hudson River, and Herbert recalled that crowds of people were waving to the prisoners of war from a bridge as the ship passed underneath[32]. Herbert thought that they might have been mistaken for returning American soliders[32]. On arrival in America they were greeted by something quite unexpected. The Americans led them into a room full of food. It was food of a quantity and quality that they had never before seen in the austere days of the war. Some of the prisoners gorged themselves, some swallowed frankfurter sausages whole.

Herbert recalled that in all of his time as a prisoner of war, he and his fellow prisoners were always treated very well by the Americans. But when he and fellow prisoners of war were taken to their prison camp, which was near Boston, they however did not receive such a warm welcome from some of the German prisoners of war who had been captured earlier in the war. Some of the longer-term German prisoners blamed the new arrivals for giving up too easily and losing the war. The new arrivals were spat upon by some of the longer-term prisoners. In some barracks the longer-term prisoners meted out even worse brutality on new arrivals. But the Nazis had been defeated and most had no time for the old order. Herbert recalled that some kind of mass fracas once blew up within the camp. A former SS officer stood upon a table and tried to quell the disturbance; from the crowd came a voice "Oh get down you golden pheasant".

During his stay near Boston, Herbert once witnessed the Northern Lights. He recalled to me the amazing sight of curtains of light moving around the sky. Around 1947, the prisoners of war began to be released or repatriated. Some of the prisoners had relatives in America: relatives who had immigrated to America from Germany many decades before. Some of the prisoners who had American relatives were given American citizenship and released into the care of their American relatives. Herbert recalls watching some of those prisoners walking out the prison gates to be picked up by American relatives in big posh cars. For Herbert and the remainder of his fellows, 1947 brought a trip back across the Atlantic. They were not told where they were headed, and when they neared the end of the voyage two converging coastlines came into view. The prisoners thought that they were on their way back to Germany and had assumed that these were the coasts of England and France, and that they were in the English Channel. In fact, the coastlines were that of the wider Mersey estuary; they were on their way to Liverpool. In England they were released into an open camp. They were free to come and go; though there were some restrictions. They were even allowed get jobs outside of the camp. They did odd jobs for folk: gardening and the like. And Herbert and his fellows found among the British people acceptance and friendliness. In all of his time in Britain, Herbert never once found resentment or bitterness from the British people.

Given the choice to go back to Germany, Herbert chose to stay in England. He got a manual job with an Army bomb disposal unit. Eventually he became a clerk for the unit and was based in Horsham in Sussex. And in this country, he made a way of life in which he found contentment. During his weekends he made trips to the south coast. During his leave periods he joined fellow cyclists and campers in the Cycling Fraternity. I knew Herbert later in his life, and he would often reflect on his years as a young man - times in his newly adopted country that were eventful and memorable.

One hot and sunny weekend in the 1950s Herbert made a trip to somewhere on the south coast. In fact, on this occasion he got a lift from a colleague. Sometime during the course of the day came an announcement over a loud hailer that a mine had been found in the sand and everyone was ordered to leave the beach. Herbert's colleague was eager to help with the situation and spoke to the police who were busy cordoning off the area. The colleague had access to an explosives store back at the camp and told the police that he had experience in the disposal of bombs; he managed to persuade the police that he could deal with this mine. Perhaps though, it was the case that the man had merely seen it done before. The colleague went away and later returned with some explosives. The police kept everyone well away while the colleague, accompanied by Herbert, proceeded to the mine. It was a small antipersonnel mine, and Herbert's colleague carefully packed the explosives around the mine. The colleague lit the fuse and Herbert and his colleague ran and then hit the sand. It was an impressive explosion which left a sizable crater in the sand. The day was saved and all were allowed to return to their weekend at the beach. On Monday morning back in the camp, Herbert's colleague reported his weekend deeds to the officer in charge. This brought great surprise and severe admonishment: The officer's eyes became wide and his face red, "You did WHAT! You did WHAT!"

Camping with the Cycling Fraternity brought Herbert to North Wales. With the fraternity he once cycled from Horsham to North Wales, camped for a week and then cycled back. Herbert it always seemed possessed boundless energy and enthusiasm for the outdoors life. In his younger years, Herbert's camping expeditions even extended into Christmas, but these were purely solitary affairs. One Christmas in the 1950s he camped at Lydd Range: this is a long stretch of coast that lies off an isolated wild expanse of shingled scrubland between Camber Sands and Dungeness. During the nighttimes he sheltered in an old Second World War bunker. By the light of his candle he remembered looking at the rough concrete ceiling above his head and thinking how cracked it looked. A few months later he read in the newspaper that some army personnel on training had been using that very same bunker. Suddenly the roof collapsed on top of them. One of the men suffered a broken pelvis.

On one Christmas holiday Herbert was sitting on the beach at Lydd Range. While heating water for some coffee on his meth's stove, he noticed a helicopter flying low along the beach toward him. The helicopter then circled him for a few minutes before departing. Soon the lone figure of a man approached him from along the empty beach. This turned out to be a policeman: "Excuse me sir, have you lost a boat?" As the policeman proceeded with his questions, Herbert noticed a little way off, a motorcycle policeman poised on the sea wall path. Herbert explained to the policeman where he was from and what he was doing on the beach, and the policeman seemed happy with that and shortly left. Herbert had been into local shops to buy provisions, and he reasoned that someone may have become suspicious of a lone man with a foreign accent camped out among the wilds. I suspect that this incident did not surprise Herbert; these were indeed the days of the Cold War.

Herbert's family lived in what became after the Second World War East Germany. During the period of the Cold War Herbert was able to make visits to his family, but these journeys were often flavoured with the signs of those times. His employment in Britain brought him good money relative to his family's income back home, and he would travel to East Germany laden with gifts. Herbert would travel by train from West to East Germany, and the transition between these two states made for anxious moments. At the border, East German guards would board the train and rigorously check the carriages. One time the guards checked Herbert's baggage. They unwrapped in their searching all of the Christmas presents that Herbert had prepared for his family. Not satisfied that they had found no contraband and seemingly insensitive to Herbert's tense predicament, they asked Herbert "If you are not hiding anything, then why are you sweating?" The guards moved on, leaving torn Christmas paper and gifts scattered untidily across the floor. The other passengers on the train helped Herbert to get it all back together again. Coming back the other way, from East to West Germany, the East German guards checked the carriages before they reached their destination in the West. Once the guards had gone, and the train had crossed into the West German state, a couple sitting opposite Herbert lifted the ashtray from its recess in the seat. They gleefully removed a load of jewellery. This was family jewellery they explained, and they were taking it to the West. If it had been found, it would have likely been confiscated.

During Herbert's visits to East Germany, as a person from the West, he was required to report to the local police station periodically. A sign of the strange days of the Cold War came by way of a curious incident on one of those visits. An official at the police station asked Herbert "Would you like to come to a party?" "Well no" replied Herbert, "I have only limited time with my family here" The official persisted with an uncompromising politeness and friendliness. "Don't worry Mr Weber we will have someone come by tonight and pick you up".

Herbert was reluctant, but back at his parent's house the family advised him that he really didn't have a choice but to go along with this "party". And sure enough a car stopped by at the house that evening and Herbert duly took the ride. They arrived at a house where someone courteously took his coat, and within the house were all the trappings of a party: there was a table with food and a large cake and copious amounts of alcoholic beverages. And there too was a room full of happy smiling guests: the friendliest of folk all wanting to meet Herbert, but none of whom Herbert had ever met. It was an uncomfortable evening for Herbert as he played along, and eventually the purpose of all of this revealed itself. He was taken to a quiet room by the host of the party, and the conversation continued "We are interested in other countries and in other cultures and how they live Mr Weber. We understand that you are working for the British Army. If there is any information that you feel might be useful, then please send it on to us".

At the end of the evening Herbert was driven back with the same sugary cordiality that had characterised this whole strange encounter. Back with his family Herbert must have breathed a big sigh of relief. But before he spoke of his experience that evening, he took off and left his coat outside - he wondered if someone had planted a bug in his coat. Back at work in England, Herbert reported this all to his superiors.

Herbert in a meadow near to the Pipes.
Photograph by Clive Tester 1979.

FINDING THE DEEP QUIET

Around 1974, at the age of eight or nine, I started to venture Under the Hill by myself. In the summer holiday of that year I had in mind to walk from Pond Hill directly across the marshes to the sea wall. For a nine-year-old it was a trek of some magnitude. Around a mile out from Pond Hill stood a small black bungalow which I used as a way mark for my route to the sea wall. It was uninhabited but looked in good repair. As the familiar landmarks of my village, the church and the radar at Allen's Hill, shrank in size so the bank of the sea wall loomed excitingly larger. And stopping to rest in the midst of the marshes I became aware of a quietness uncommon in the world from which I had come. So quiet in fact, that the subtleties of the wind whistling through the grass was the only sound. Here was a place for me, far yonder, where the wind blew its gentle way far beyond the complexities of the world.

I reached my goal: the sea wall and the vast estuary beyond. A new smell greeted me as I stepped through the foliage on the tidal saltings: the sweet smell of salt marsh flora filled the summer air. Spicy almost to the point of pungency, it gave a surprise to the senses that might have been a caution from this quiet realm into which my clumsy boots had encroached.

Seeking the tranquillity that the quiet marshes provided took me on many such solitary walks through my boyhood years. Though I would not be entirely alone on the marshes. Many a time I would meet Jack Baxter the Shepherd from Boatwick House. Over the years from boyhood and into adulthood I would oftentimes see Jack on my walks, as he tended to his sheep, and we would speak about what was afoot on the marshes. Jack's childhood was on the marshes around Colchester, and as a child he had an affinity for the outdoor life; Jack would have understood what drew me always to the marshes[28]. Jack as with all of the Cliffe farmers would always be graciously forbearing of my childhood ventures.

A Chatham Rochester and Gillingham News article from the early 1960s courtesy of Ken and Carol Baxter gives some background into Jack's work on the marshes. Jack tended up to 1500 sheep on 400 acres of Cliffe marshes and was secretary of the Hundred of Hoo Sheepdog club. Jack was a skilful trainer of sheepdogs. His best sheepdog was a border collie called Rover, and with Rover Jack won cups throughout the county.

The newspaper article shows how shepherds like Jack trained the sheepdogs, a technique requiring dedication and great patience. From the article:

The dog is first let out into the open and allowed to move wherever he wants. When he starts to go left, the left command is shouted - in Jack Baxter's case "Way on". If he goes right, the command "Go by" is shouted. In the same way, whatever the dog does, the appropriate command is given. When the dog obeys the voice command almost automatically, then the handler can use a special 5-way dog whistle. After a voice command he blows a certain note, and so the dog begins to associate the whistle with the type of command.

Today, Jack's son Ken and his wife Carol and their family keep the family tradition of sheep farming alive, running a sheep farm from Boatwick House.

UNDER THE FERAL WOOD

Drawn by the promise of mystery and adventure, Under the Hill was also a place of shared adventure with my school friends and I. Around 1975 we discovered up on the hill above Pickles Way a curious bowl-shaped depression in the ground known to us as the Bird's Nest. Of firm compacted soil it was the shape and size of one of those large circular Jacuzzis that you often find in holiday parks. It became a regular place for us; it was our haunt. I often used to wonder whether the Bird's Nest was a remnant of an earlier structure, perhaps ancient, because of its symmetrical form. There is a local report that it was used as a gun emplacement during world war two[33]. There our gang would gather: Adrian Hatcher, David Arnold, Martin Bishop, John Rodford, Mark Long, Paul Enticknap, David Read, Stephen Knight, Dave Esler, Graham Faulkner and more.

From the Bird's Nest we would make our ways to the Track negotiating our way down the cliffs by way of well trodden paths; one such path we knew as the Elephant's Trunk. Always it seemed that however well we thought we knew the intricacies of our treasured quarry the Track oftentimes revealed to us something of enchantment. The Track was full of hidden recesses; many of them introduced to us by my older brother Clifford. Adrian and I recall a time when Clifford took us to the chimney foundations of the Francis Chamber Kiln. A half-century before, my uncles George, Eddie and Sid had stood in that very same place to gaze up through the high chimney that once towered above the chamber kilns. By the late 20th century all that remained of that chimney was the deep hole of its gaping foundation. The leafy pit was hidden beneath a dense wood, and only a privileged few knew of it. Around the periphery of the chimney foundation were the entry points of a number of flues; the brickwork of the flues was splendidly curved and symmetrical and very pleasing to the eye. At the bottom of the pit we clambered our way over a mound of moss-covered bricks and into the old access tunnel where we ventured into the deep silent blackness at the heart of the chamber kiln. Retracing our steps, we emerged back into daylight and ventured out into the wooded quarry and its labyrinthine tracks. Through its seemingly impenetrable foliage we came across a small clearing. There, captured in a chink of sunshine amid the green twilight beneath the feral wood, stood a single bright orchid[33].

Close to the chimney foundations this structure is a flue through which hot gasses from the drying chambers were fed into the base of the main chimney. It is hidden deep within the thicket on top of the Francis Chamber Kiln. Many such structures like this are evident in the chamber kiln remnants.

Photograph by Clive Tester 1983.

The Francis Chamber Kiln had become known to our generation of the 1970s as the Arches. This was in reference to the supporting arch structures visible on its southern face. Most of the kiln complex was concealed and forever hidden from the sun behind a thick hawthorn and birch wood. From the dampened soil of this vast thicket, rope like vines of bramble and old man's beard reached up into the darkened tree canopy grasping for the sunlight. Further into the thicket the ground beneath our feet crunched with old kiln cinders. Here, tall buttresses of Victorian concrete evoked images of ancient stone between which curious portals of smoke-tinged concrete led into yawning kilns. Long before our time, in the years before our parents were born, here once laid the last dying embers of a great factory of old; the likes of which had brought many of the old names to Cliffe. Now within those old furnaces cool bracken sprouted from the crumbling mortar between its heat-mottled firebricks.

"Beneath the feral wood". One of the concrete buttresses and an opening into one of the kilns at the south-western end of the Francis Chamber Kiln built before 1897. Photographs by Clive Tester 1983.

View from the north-western end of the Francis Chamber Kiln. The opening into one of the kilns built in or after 1897 (left), and a concrete buttress of the pre-1897 structure (right). Photographs by Adrian Hatcher 2015.

This wonderfully vast and hidden complex of kilns reminded me of paperback adventure stories of machete clad explorers rediscovering ancient cities lost to the deep dark rainforest. It was the character of the Arches that was captured in the imagination and expressed in the wild animated humour of Martin Bishop. We'd often be rummaging around in our explorations when a deep voice would echo forth from the thicket. We'd turn around to find Martin in David Bellamy character sat among the undergrowth with arms outstretched to the luxuriant flora all around him: *"Here I am under the canopy of this vast rainforest"* Grasping a handful of leafy humus and casting it passionately into the air *"This RICH soil is home to this truly amazing variety of plants"*. Martin was a great laugh as the archetypal Botanic Man.

Known to only a few of us was a row of arches deep within the thicket of the kiln's north-western end; we knew that series of arches as Ken's Caves. This row of arches was likely of the original pre-1897 structure and is partly covered at their base by the kilns added in or after 1897. The arched entrances to Ken's Caves were difficult to reach through the prickly brambles that veiled them. However, we would clamber with ease down a hole into the back of one of the caverns below. The cave seemed to exist in a strange stasis and permanently fixed in a time that bore little correlation with the fast-changing age beyond the bounds of Under the Hill. Ingrained in the cold cement surface of the cave were wood grain patterns imprinted from the rafters on which the concrete arch was cast back in the time when Victoria reigned. From the concave roof hung mini lime stalactites quietly growing in infinitesimal time from a slow diffusion of water born of the dampened soil above. A peculiar little plant grew in small lonely cliques from the bare soil of the caves; it personified the place. Of dark green crinkled edged leaves, it grew only in the humid eternal shade of the caves that had not known the wind or the rain in generations. It seemed to know no seasons, taking its life force from the eerie unchanging ambiance of the caves. It was so odd to see it growing here so far from the sun, its strange leaves never to be moved by any wind. This static little plant was uncanny, and we avoided it, almost as if it harboured a strange quiet watchful sentience. And as our teenage years progressed toward adulthood, through hot summers and snow-hardened winters, the shadow plants seemed neither to grow nor wilt. The life of the shadow plants, like the stalactites above us, existed within a timescale of which we could barely conceive through the eager pace of our teenage years.

Our hidden entrance down into Ken's Caves. Photograph by Adrian Hatcher 2015.

I believe that the real essence of a place like the Track exists most truly in our perceptions. Adrian and I often reflect on a fleeting moment at Ken's Caves back in the spring of 1980 which has come to define the sense of mystique the Track will always hold for us: Adrian and I call it the Whistler. Of the five of us, only Adrian and I heard it: a short tin-whistle like song playing forth from the depths of the thicket behind Ken's Caves. There was clarity to those notes which made the Whistler appear to be very close by indeed. But so deep and impenetrable was the thicket that we would never discover from whom this little tune came. It was unusual, as Adrian recalls it was very strange but not scary. The truth behind the Whistler is likely prosaic, but it serves as a useful allegory for something both splendid and hidden. For Adrian and I, a sense of the mystical was conveyed through that brief little melody. It was as if an apparition was brought forth from that strange and wonderful parallel time inhabited by our orchid secreted in its glade of light and the patient shadow plants of our caves of mossy concrete. The origin of the Whistler we shall never know, but maybe there was an element of providence at play here. One of the most artistic in our school year, Adrian I believe is very receptive to the sense of the extraordinary; it is a heightened awareness that is coupled with his natural artistic flair. It is an artistic talent that finds expression in many ways, in his painting and photography. Of our days Under the Hill and in the times since, this creative flair often found expression too in a convivial quick wit of surreal humour that precisely captures the character of the world around us.

Back in the village, the youth club and the pubs to where we had started to venture became an important part of our social scene. There, we would meet new friends and characters like Darren Gee, Graham Levy, Mark Pope, Dave Stammers, Andy Simpson AKA "Simmone", Gordon Hacker, and Chris Hill AKA "Grunt". Grunt had a great sense of humour; our evenings with Grunt were jovial cheerful times of laughter. We all missed Grunt when he died in a road accident in 1981.

And all the while, Under the Hill remained special as we grew into our later teenage years. The marshes, in particular the Francis Chalk Quarry, was regarded as a kind of sacred place for us. On autumn days a little wood fire might cast our shadows onto the arced walls of Ken's Caves. Sometimes Under the Hill would make a suitably secluded location for the euphoria of cider. Our conversations would then flow in an uninhibited stream of consciousness, frequently turning to the things of our age. We shared concerns of the wider world of which we were becoming increasingly aware. For this was the age of the Cold War, and that was a strange time in which to grow. Some years earlier, the world stood on the brink of annihilation as the Cuban Missile Crisis unfolded. My father related to me once, how during the Cuban Missile Crisis he had gone to bed at night wondering whether there would still be a world outside when he woke the next day. We lived in a unique age defined by mistrust between nations of contrasting ideologies. And this was the nuclear age, where a single thermonuclear bomb, of which those nations possessed thousands, could crush an entire region. That was the reality of a future the world might face. The screening of The War Game at Hoo School in the early 1980s only reinforced that awareness for us. Should "the button be pressed", all that we knew would in an instant turn to ash, and not even deep within the seclusion of Ken's Caves would we find protection from the all-consuming cosmic heat of the Cold War turned hot.

The Francis Chamber Kiln known to us as the Arches photographed from the chalk hill to the west. Photograph by Clive Tester January 1979.

The pre-1897 kilns of The Francis Chamber Kiln complex. Evident in the photograph on the left are sheets of corrugated iron of which many still exist in the slurry drying chamber areas of the kiln complex. It appears that the slurry drying chambers were supported with corrugated iron. Photographs by Clive Tester 1983.

THE ETERNAL BLUE SKY OF 1976

It might have been one of the last rain showers that we had that side of spring. Strong sunlight and a keen wind followed a brief squall of rain that dried rapidly on the face of Gorilla's Hill. The heavy raindrops had fashioned the sandy clay of Gorilla's into friable agglomerates that reminded me of ball bearings. On days like these, the youth of the village would oftentimes gather around Percy's and Gorilla's, eager for excitement. On that day or other days like it, we of the "Birds Nest Gang" gathered along with a few more, to name but a few: Trevor and Keith Beagley; Pete and Gary Read; Paul and Mark Bishop; John Wassell; Neil Flook; Alan, Robert and Graham Bush; Andrew Slater; Lee Smith; Peter Osenton; Peter, Geoff and Paul Moore; Brian, Kevin and Phillip Edwards; Neil Henry; Paul Hunt; Adam Hunt; Mark Neal and Lee Arthur. We found among the undergrowth the engine bonnet of a plastic pig, a remnant of an old banger that had done its turn down the Track. With these and other improvised sledges we dared, and we did toboggan down the two sides of Gorilla's. The speed was exhilarating; we flew down the steep faces of Gorilla's cheering, and fearless of the tree stumps and thorny bushes that might make for painful obstacles. And sometimes these speed runs indeed ended in calamity. On more than one occasion in my boyhood such escapades concluded for me in a rapidly rolling vista of blue sky – dusty ground and blue sky over and over all the way down to the grassy plane. In the years of our boyhood that stretched before us, the Track would provide a venue for so many such escapades. And among the boys who ventured Under the Hill existed a shared sense of adventure where petty feuds and divisions were forgotten. We would explore its dense woodland, finding bullets and mortars left over from the time when the Francis Chalk Quarry was used for army training in World War Two.

For Adrian, the summer holidays of 1976 began with a motorcycle mishap down the Track. On the first day of the holidays he fell off of a friend's Honda 50 and ended up "mummified at the doctor's". In a later year David Arnold had his first ride on a motorbike: a Puch Maxi. "Close the bleedin' throttle down!" haled Adrian. It was too late, and Arn sailed right through a hedge.

A similar boyhood escapade in 1976 or '77 will always stand out in my mind as a salutary lesson in caution. We were all gathered around Percy's Hill, and I decided to take a fast-wild bicycle ride around the Track. I came to the top of Cliff Face, I'd had in mind to descend it for some time – Well I had seen Eric do this with ease so many times on his Matchless, and sometimes with me as pillion. And I had a hero in Evel Knevel too; around that time Evel was frequently seen on TV performing some spectacular stunt: jumping vast canyons in rocket cars and rows of London busses on a motorbike. So, without a second thought I descended, accelerating at an alarming rate down the near vertical chalk bank. And as soon as I had started, a kind of resonant motion began in the small light front wheel of the bicycle that seemed to amplify with every foot that the bike descended. The oscillations propagated through the entire frame until I was launched over the handlebars long before I had reached the bottom. I picked myself up with not a scratch or bruise, bizarrely unhurt. And most importantly, no one had been around Cliff Face to witness my humiliating calamity. I returned to my group of friends who were still gathered at Percy's. It was clear to me by their amusement that they all knew some mishap had occurred. It took someone to point out to me that the back of my trousers and underpants had a long clean rip from top to bottom.

As the summer heat of 1976 grew, the focus of our leisure time was swimming in the clay lakes that we knew as the Pontoons, the Crystal and Swan Lake. My father had bought a large inflatable dingy. Of a weekend evening we would drive down Pond Hill and to the Pontoons, to the first of the lakes along the road. My father and all of us brothers would row out to the middle of the lake and then dive into the water for a long evening swim.

In my final year at Cliffe School in 1976, come home time I sprang forth. Eager for open-air freedom, my friends and I would cycle or sometimes run to the Crystal. Black Lane from the bottom of Allen's Hill and all the way through to Quarry Cottages was a shady tunnel through a thick canopy of tall trees. The path was made up of local material: rounded flint and kiln cinders and it was firm underfoot. Further down, past Quarry Cottages, oddments of its past industry were evident in the path: heavy bolts among other pieces of ironwork in all probability from the Francis days. At Quarry Cottages, we could take one of two routes to the Crystal. If we were on bikes, then we would cycle along Creek Road until we got to the Wellcome Yacht Club where we crossed a sturdy wooden bridge and on to a path that led to the Crystal. But if we left our bikes at home, we could take a significant short cut. Following Black Lane to the petrol storage depot, we would turn west and to the Pipes. Here the petroleum pipeline that lay buried along the length of the path to the Crystal was exposed as they crossed a narrow stretch of the lake. There was one large diameter and two smaller pipes spanning forty or so feet. The pipes were sturdy enough to be used as a bridge by all and sundry, being supported by suspension cables anchored to both banks.

It was my brother Clifford or one of his contemporaries who coined the name "the Crystal" in the early 1970s. During the 1970s the water of these freshly dug clay lakes was reasonably clear. Before the 1970s the focus of swimming at Cliffe had been largely at the Creek[16]. With the closure of the Alpha, the clay lakes on the marshes became popular for swimmers, not having the inconvenience of low tide. These were long and energetic days of swimming in the sun where I would be joined by friends to name: Alec Pennell, Paul Hunt, Andrew Slater, Paul Enticknap, Tony Jeffrey and others. In later years to come we would be joined by Robert Cox, Andrew Penniall and also by Shaun Hutchings of Cliffe Woods and Peter Rolland of High Halstow. The younger among us though would only go in the water when Herbert or the older boys were around to look out for us. We would drift around exploring the lake in that big old rowboat left over from the days of the pontoon cranes. Sometimes we would all go over to the Creek, and at low tide lark in the mud, then back to the Crystal to wash it all off. Some of the older boys would turn up on their track bikes, and some even in cars. There were always plenty of pranks. While one lad was swimming, some of the others packed his crash helmet with dried cowpats!

One time we turned up at the Crystal, and a diving board had been built by some of the older boys. It was a fine example of civil engineering from local resources; it had been built from driftwood of the Creek. Whoever built it had some talent and must have gone far. Constructed level with the high bank above the Crystal, it must have been ten feet above the water, and long enough to take a good run so that we would fly through the hot summer air.

In the warm evening we would walk home sometimes stopping at Quarry Cottages for a drink of water courtesy of Sis and Bert Hoare. We would walk up Black Path and at the back of the old dairy at Allen's Hill was a tap where we could take a drink. Then onto Buttway Lane where a row of big old elm trees stood near to the corner with West Street. The tree at the corner had a cave in its trunk big enough to swallow two children. Back at Rookery Crescent, Nationwide was on the television while our mum cooked our tea. In the evening after a day's work running the Post Office and then being there for us, our mum would sometimes play Paul Robeson on the record player in the front room. Old Man River spoke of a wise old river that just kept rolling on and transcending the tribulations of the world. Those songs recorded back when my mother was a child were deeply reflective. Songs like Water Boy and Old Man River sang in Paul Robeson's baritone voice had a real resonance with me.

My brother Clifford got his first job in 1976 working on the Arco Thames gravel dredger that operated out in the North Sea. The summer holidays were now here and on days when the Arco Thames was due to dock at Cliffe Fort, I would wait up on top of the cliffs at the Track until the distinctive form of the vessel appeared along the river. I would run down to the Fort to meet him. In the days of Clifford's leave, we would walk to the Crystal with friends including Martyn Smith and Stephen Holbourn. There we would meet with others for leisure, relaxation and swimming to name: Ken Baxter, David Slater, Andy Chilcott, Jim Ebbs, Neil Watkins, Wayne Harrison, Phillip and Kevin Edwards. Clifford had a tape recorder on which he'd recorded some of our mum's Paul Robeson songs. On those sultry summer days, the cool enclosure of trees that flanked Black Lane would resonate with the haunting tones of Paul Robeson as we passed through. For me, to this day, those lingering songs evoke memories of that long hot summer at the Crystal, of bare feet on hot sun-baked ground in a meadow of radiant golden grass, of the deep earthy aroma of ancient clay the banks of which descended to the deep clear water of the Crystal.

My brothers Eric (nearest to the camera) and Clifford (middle), at the Crystal in the early 1970s. Photograph by Herbert Weber.

Clifford (nearest to the camera) and Eric at the Crystal in the early 1970s. Photograph by Herbert Weber.

On the banks of the Crystal in the early 1970s: Clifford, Andy Chilcott and Phillip Edwards (closest to the camera) Photograph by Herbert Weber.

I once swam over to the southern bank of the Crystal near to the County Wall to find a mound of corrugated iron: the remains of the shepherd's wick from the days when sheep grazed the field that became the Crystal. Along the southern bank of the Crystal ran the track of the County Wall. It was an old potholed clay track, and there was an old wooden gate at the County Wall's northern end. That gate was there probably since the days when Dick Dowsett's father was a shepherd on these marshes. That was of the time before the war when a vast wet reed field to the west existed untamed. It was the time when the land of our lakes was being forged; a time that held a special allure for me; for those days were the very depth of this land. And while those days seemed incredibly distant to me, the character of that time was palpably present at the

Crystal. It was there in that olden farm gate, it was there in the remains of the old shepherd's wick, and it was there in a clay pipe that I found in the waters below the old tramway. It was a time closer to the heart of this landscape, our landscape that gave us such reflection and freedom. The Crystal is my very own Old Man River; the Crystal will forever be my old friend.

The Crystal. Photographs by Clive Tester circa 1985.

SILOS IN THE MIST

The summer of 1977 was cool by contrast to the classic 1976, though the misty marshes of a summer holiday morning has left a charm to my memories of that summer.

I woke to find a thick mist had drifted in overnight from the North Sea to fill the lowlands of the Thames Estuary. The fog lingered into midmorning as my friends and I: Lee Smith, Paul Bishop, Mark Bishop, John Wassell, Neil Flook and Bob Rayfield made our way Under the Hill. The fog gave us a different perspective on the land that day: our land was transformed into a world in splendid isolation. Ours was a world of dew coated trees amid meadows of tall grasses that stretched out to the infinity of the fog; the only sound in that world was the occasional hoot of a distant ship. Onward we ambled, onward onto the narrow wooden bridge at the eastern end of the Crystal. We joked and we larked, and in the thick still air we jumped and dived from the bridge. The waves of our play radiated forth across the quiet calm water to ultimately vanish into the mist that encircled us. Beyond our cocoon of fog was but one looming vision: the vast silhouette of the Alpha; its silos and chimneys stood grey against grey like a giant shadow cast upon our sky. And through a distortion of perspective born of the hazy air the lone silo block, the tallest of all, seemed to be vast in a manner wholly beyond the realms of the marshes we knew. There in the diffuse light it stood; cast in concrete smooth and sheer; like a mountain booming deep into the sky above our sea of mist.

That was a powerful image of the Alpha which has remained to this day etched in my memory. It was an image that captured my imagination and my interest; it filled me with a sense of intrigue as to what might lay within the Alpha's sheds of creosoted wood and cement encrusted corrugated iron. From that day, I would seek the history of the industry of our village by drawing on the memories of the old folk of Cliffe, all of whom were generous with their memories. And I would find a special link to that past industry in a family who had for over a century lived among and worked in the cement industry of Cliffe Marshes. From my earliest days spent Under the Hill with my friends and family, we had oftentimes dropped by for a glass of water at the home of Burt and Sis Hoare. We were always welcome at Quarry Cottages.

QUARRY COTTAGES

Burt Hoare was a truly affable man, and he was always pleased to see me and to talk about the days of old. Burt's working life had been on the pontoon cranes of the marshes, and he spoke fondly in his recollections of those days. Those were the times when Aunt Sis hung a tea towel in the upstairs window of Quarry Cottages to signify the mid day meal to the men working on the pontoon cranes. I was fascinated with that era before my time; Bert's life working among the clay lakes of the marshes seemed idyllic to me. Sadly, Burt passed away in 1978.

From the mid 1970s my friendship with Aunt Sis grew. After school and at weekends I would visit. We sat for many hours in the living room of Quarry Cottages speaking of olden times. I gained an insight into Aunt Sis' strongly independent character. I sensed that her social norms were firmly grounded in the Edwardian era of her formative years; norms quite different from those that seemed to prevail by the 1970s. While politically conservative, Aunt Sis was respectful of the labour leanings of my growing political awareness. Aunt Sis was of strong Christian faith; a faith that I have grown to know and to understand more deeply as my years have progressed.

Quarry Cottages presented a cosy setting. The horsehair and lime plastering of its rooms[1] were decorated with flowery wallpaper. When Bert and Sis first came to live at Quarry Cottages sometime between the first and second world wars the lighting had been from oil lamps[1]. By my time in the 1970s the oil lamps had been replaced by gas lighting. Lighting for the living room was from two thorium gas lamps mounted on the wall above the fireplace. The gas was supplied from bottled gas which was kept in the adjacent kitchen; a copper gas pipe linked the living room lights to the kitchen. Bottled gas was also used to run a small fridge in the kitchen. A portable black and white television resided in the living room; it was powered from a car battery. Quarry Cottages were never connected to mains power or mains gas.

The windows of the living room looked out upon the back garden. Something quite curious and a little spooky used to happen when a tug or ship came along the river a mile to the north. Through the quietness of the house could be heard a steady vibration in one of the windows. While the sound of the heavy boat engine at that distance was too low for the human ears, it did however set up an audible resonance in that one window. By my time, a dense hawthorn wood had encroached into much of the garden of Quarry Cottages. The wood made for a haven for wildlife. Aunt Sis would often relate to me of the scene that greeted her when she opened the curtains of a morning: alone in the serenity of the morning stillness, a Robin darting from twig to twig. She once had the privilege to glimpse the face of a badger in the hawthorn thicket. Aunt Sis' garden was magical in late winter: snowdrops abound in the lawn around her concrete fish pond. The fish pond she would clean regularly even when turning 80. The garden was well-kept, and it was bordered in places with rows of cement testing briquettes from the Alpha.

Aunt Sis had many visitors who gave me much insight into the cement industry. Her wider family often visited. They were a family integral to the cement industry of Cliffe with men like Eric Slater who had worked on the pontoon cranes. Aunt Sis' brother, George Slater, lived at Pond Hill. George had worked as a coke boy at the Francis Chamber Kiln just the other side of Black Lane to Quarry Cottages. George in the late 1970s took me on a tour of the kiln complex where he had worked as a boy. George showed me the flint wall of the embankment that flanks the kilns. Upon the embankment, still in place under a layer of leaf mould, lay a row of railway sleepers upon which rested the rails of the railway that delivered coke to the kilns. From the embankment, George would lift baskets of coke the twenty or so feet to the top of the kilns. George and his workmates would load coke into the top of the kilns.

It was at Quarry Cottages that I became acquainted with Jack Sullivan. Jack did many odd jobs for Aunt Sis: delivering her groceries and also charging her television battery at his home. Jack had been an engineer at the Alpha. Born in 1910, Jack had an early memory of the First World War period of hearing the booming sound of a Zeppelin's unbalanced engines from the direction of the Thames estuary. I had a few walks around Cliffe marshes with Jack. He was able to add context to many of the relics I had found in our landscape. For example, I had often wondered about the huge pile of twisted reinforced concrete in the mudflats in front of Cliffe Fort. It turns out that these are the remains of a second World War fortification once erected many miles out in the Thames Estuary. It was towed back up the Thames after the war and deposited at Cliffe. I found Jack interesting and I felt that we had some things in common. Jack was passionate about worker's rights and the right of public access to the land. Jack was a champion of local footpaths, a cause to which I would follow in his footsteps.

Another frequent visitor to Aunt Sis who I had the privilege to befriend was Percy Payne of Kitcheners Road Strood. Percy had a deep interest in Cliffe Marshes, its history, its wildlife and its environment. Percy was an affable and a fascinating man with a broad knowledge of the ancient history of the area. I knew Percy in his retirement years. He was in his 70s when he would come to Cliffe Marshes often digging for ancient relics in the mudflats of Cliffe and Higham creeks. Percy had worked as a kiln burner at the cement factories of the Medway. From Aunt Sis, Jack Sullivan and Percy Payne, I learned most of what I understand about the process of lime and cement manufacture.

One of my school friends Billy Simmons often visited; like me Billy had a keen interest in the history of our area. Sometimes of a Sunday morning, Ray Francis would visit. Ray was from an old Cliffe family with strong links to the local industry: Ray's father had been a train driver in the Francis Chalk Quarry.

Between the late 70s and early 80s I made almost daily visits to Quarry Cottages. Aunt Sis once took me up the steep and narrow stairs to the top room of the cottages. The room was perfectly square, and the high easterly facing window afforded a view to the flat horizon of the greater Thames estuary. That day, an inky shower cloud towered above the horizon over the estuary from which fell a dark curtain of icy rain.

The darkened land before us stood out in shadowy stark contrast: a prelude to a heavy downfall.

Back downstairs, Aunt Sis brought tea from the kitchen which we drank by the crackling coal fire in the living room. Aunt Sis spoke of the far distant times when her parents were alive. Back in the days when her father would pay a visit, Aunt Sis would catch the rich tobacco scent of her father's clay pipe long before he came to the door. Now turning 80, Aunt Sis would sometimes catch the same smoky scent just as if her father was walking up the garden path to visit her.

While we had talked, the rain curtain had swept across the vast estuary to Egypt Bay and from there across the marshes to the pontoon lakes and on toward Quarry Cottages. My ears were drawn from the gentle crackle of the fire to the sound of heavy raindrops bouncing at the window. Outside in the rain darkened air, the thicket of Black Lane seemed haunted by an aura: a misty purple hue as deep and curious as the hidden relics of another age now safely concealed beneath leaf mould of half a century. In a while the sun began to shine on the cliffs of the Francis Chalk Quarry. Those relics were waiting patiently for me and to there I was drawn to explore - to the old quarry I took a walk.

Within an area of dense hawthorn close to the Black Lane well was a hidden glade. It may have been known only to my brothers and I; Clifford had taken me there a few years earlier. It was a little patch of healthy grass in the order of six by twelve feet. Kept trim by rabbits, it was a lawn of a quality that any gardener would have been proud. That glade was a hidden magical place; it existed in pristine isolation. I almost felt like removing my shoes before I walked upon its fine grass. Within the wider thicket beyond the glade existed small clearings where white violets flowered in springtime. And among that thicket too could be found a line of railway sleepers which ran in the direction to Black Path. At the bottom of Black Path neat contours were discernible in the path where sleepers once lay. The ghostly imprint of the old railway line continued around the cliffs of the Picnic Grounds. Those cliffs, discoloured in places with soot deposits from the age of steam, still bore the pick marks of the manual chalk diggers of old. And in the thick grass on the cliff tops I would find metal spikes driven into the ground where long ago those chalk digger's ropes were secured. Beneath the steep bank at the bottom of Black Path lay the old riveted iron chimney of the steam engine of Aunt Sis' childhood days. The chimney lay next to a curious brick structure now in the permanent damp and mossy shade beneath the wood: a relic from a different age when the quarry was bare and bustling.

I would return the next day to Aunt Sis to hear her reminisce of the days when these relics were part of a busy factory that she walked past on her way to school. Back in Aunt Sis' early years living at Cliffe Creek the river was a lively place too. Back in the early 1900s, dolphins were often seen in the Thames at Cliffe. The river was a busy place for industry and shipping with much greater activity than today. And sometimes a body would be found along the shore. Back in those days, Aunt Sis' brothers would be paid to bring a body from the shore in a wheel barrow to the Charnel House at Cliffe Church.

And Aunt Sis often spoke of the quiet magic that this land now held in its post-industrial era. She told of what she once saw and heard one morning in a little silver birch cops close to the old slurry backs in the Francis Chalk Quarry while walking her dog Butch. I can imagine today the enchanting winter dawn Aunt Sis witnessed that day:

The dormancy of winter lay all around and everything within the little copse, isolated as it was among the white chalk cliffs, shone with the fresh sparkle of winter hoarfrost. Its crystalline purity enveloped all: from the leaf-covered ground to the extremities of every tree and glittered with innumerable points of light in the first rays of the morning sun. The frost conveyed a clean and fresh icy purity, born of an all-consuming chill, that found expression too in the sky where even the brightest stars had disappeared at first light when the cold dark of night subsided before the bright though equally harsh violet blue dawn.

Faint though it was, a gentle wraithlike jingle could be heard scarcely above the morning silence; a sound so slight that it would have gone unnoticed but for the deep peace of the quarry and the remote marsh beyond. Likewise, the delicate wisp of a breeze that caused the fragile icicles of frost to whisper would have remained unnoticed too, but for the ethereal melody of magical notes that their chafing produced.

A winter's day in the Picnic Grounds

Our conversation oftentimes continued beyond sunset and I would come away after dark. On parting Aunt Sis would always say "Remember me to your parents". Walking back along Black Lane the living room window of Quarry Cottages glowed by the light of the gas lamp. Glancing back occasionally, the retreating light seemed ever bright amid the deep darkness through which I could barely see my feet. The village was a mile yonder and before me and on each side lay the silence of the shadowy thicket. If there were any ghosts here in the darkness they were from those distant times of Aunt Sis' childhood that had become the focus of my obsession. Gazing into the undergrowth I hoped that for a brief moment space and time might yield to my desire to glimpse the incandescent heat of those kilns of olden days.

Quarry Cottages in 1978. This photograph was given to me by Aunt Sis.

THE SILENT ALPHA

By the end of 1978 word was around that the Alpha was due for demolition. I felt that it was imperative to capture the spirit of the Alpha as it was before the demolition team moved in. And so, I took it upon myself to explore its realm. In February 1979 with camera in hand I took a walk along Salt Lane to the old factory.

Two photographs that show just how close the Alpha was to Concrete Cottages and the Royal Albert Pub. Photographs by Clive Tester 1979.

There was a special kind of stillness to be found within the bounds of the Alpha; it possessed a peculiar kind of quietness that I found profoundly alluring. It was stillness and calm that was brought into clear sharp focus by a sense of contrast. Here before me stood three rotary kilns long as a playing field. Those huge tunnels of steel and firebrick once rotated on powerful cogs and rollers while an inferno roared inside. I recall that painted in neat letters on the motors that once kept the kilns in motion was the last service date - 1967. The kiln doors were open. I could peer right down into the blackness where once had been a tunnel of spinning glowing incandescent heat. The kilns had rested cold for a decade, motionless in darkened silence. Yet a ghost of their time lingered: a hint of fiery coal haunted the air. The inner workings of the factory were still intact. In the vast clinker shed lay the ball mills that once ground clinker and crushed coal. Their dormant power was palpable in their big motors of chunky iron construction; now they slept beneath a veil of rust.

The three rotary kilns of the Alpha. Photograph by Clive Tester 1979.

Fine cement dust of six decades had accumulated in every recess of the factory, sculptured by the prevailing air currents into smooth snow-like drifts. The towering silos, which once held thousands of tons of cement, were now the empty cavernous shells of a great industry now past. The iron gantries and walkways high up on the silos reminded me of the gantries of the Saturn launch tower of the Apollo era; heavy engineering that spoke of energy of a kind that fascinates and inspires. Within the factory on a workbench lay an old newspaper dated November 1969. Flicking through I came to the TV page; Apollo 12 featured on all three channels. Like Apollo, the Alpha belonged to an age that brought nostalgia to me. It was of the time of my very earliest memories, the time when men once travelled between worlds. That time now seemed as distant and as magical to me as the Moon that Apollo once visited. Yet here within the realms of the Alpha I had a sense that time had stopped in that era and that those silos still held the atmosphere of April 1st 1970.

Silo number 2 at the Alpha. Photograph by Clive Tester 1979.

Chimneys 1 and 2 at the Alpha. Photograph by Clive Tester 1979.

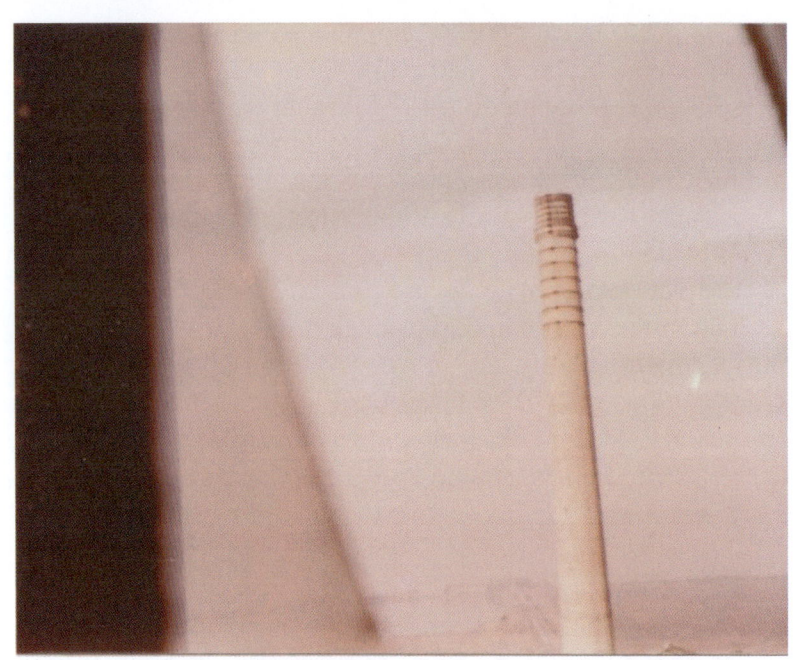

Chimney number 3 at the Alpha viewed from the packing shed of silo number 1. Photograph by Clive Tester 1979.

Along with the yellowing newspaper, laying upon the workbench was a rusting cat food tin. From across the kiln hall I'd catch a glimpse of a feral cat watching me from afar. Ancestors from the days of the Alpha, the cats moved as silently as spectres throughout the old factory.

At the northern most part of the factory stood a single storey building that had been the canteen. Once its steamy aromatic air would have been alive with the conversation of the Alpha workers. Now only the sound of my footsteps echoed from its cold chequered-tiled floor.

Fascinating as my foray into the Alpha had been, it would not have met with my parent's approval and certainly not to the approval of the warden Derek Hill. Derek caught me emerging from the factory, and in his most forthright manner he made it clear that it was not a place for me to be. I heeded to Derek's valid point, and to that good man's memory I say thanks for his caution and sorry for my incursion and for the concern that it must have caused.

By spring the demolition team had moved in, and the infrastructure of the Alpha was removed throughout 1979.

Removal of the rotary kilns at the Alpha. Photographs by Clive Tester 1979.

Rotary kiln with firebrick lining at the Alpha. Photograph by Clive Tester 1979.

Removal of the rotary kilns at the Alpha. The arrow in the right hand picture points to the clinker shed. Photographs by Clive Tester 1979.

By the end of the year only the three chimneys and the silo blocks remained. I recorded in my diary the events around the demolition of the chimneys and the silos:

On the 16th December 1979 came the demolition of the tallest two chimneys. I recorded in my diary that it was a bright sunny morning with a fresh moderate wind. I arrived early that morning to find the workmen drilling holes into the base of the two chimneys. Later Herbert arrived, and we observed the workmen placing explosives into the holes and then plugging the holes with cement. The charges were wired to a junction box. Herbert and I had a drink in the Royal Albert Pub. There were many people in the pub and the excited talk was of the impending demolition. When we came back outside, the workmen were placing some old iron sheets around the base of the chimneys for blast protection. We sat waiting for the time of the demolition, and over the next hour hundreds of people joined us sitting on the stationary Brett conveyor belt at a safe distance away. At 14.30, three hoots came from an air horn, then a loud and penetrating explosion was heard. As the chimneys began to fall, a series of camera clicks could be heard from the multitude. The chimneys fell and a heavy cloud of dust rose and drifted over the clay lakes. When the dust had dispersed the workmen quickly moved among the rubble to remove the copper lightning conductors, this was put under lock and key. Outside of the old Alpha reception building, Derek Hill shook hands with one of the demolition team; they seemed relieved.

The Alpha, 16th December 1979.

Left photograph: With the kilns and the clinker shed now removed, only the chimneys and silos remain. Silo number 1 is in full view, with the packing shed adjoined (see arrow). Photograph by Clive Tester.
Right photograph: At the moment of detonation a shock wave dislodged dust from the top of one of the chimneys. Photograph by Stephen Holbourn.

The chimneys fall. Photograph by Stephen Holbourn. To allow me an unrestricted view of the moment Stephen Holbourn took these photos for me and capturing the instant of detonation and the chimneys falling seconds later.

The last remaining chimney, which had been the smallest of the three, was demolished with the use of explosives on Monday the 18th February 1980 at 11.10 am. The chimney fell largely intact. Looking at the fallen chimney, I could see that it was constructed of a thick reinforced concrete outer shell with a brick lining.

Sunday March 2nd 1980 brought the demolition of the tallest of the silos. I recorded in my diary that these stood only 35 feet to the north of the Royal Albert, so it was a skilful demolition. Upon arrival that morning, my main concern was for the many pigeons which nested in the building at the top of the silo block. Herbert and I waited along with reporters and hundreds of others. At 14.00 the explosives were detonated, and immediately a huge flock of pigeons rose from the top of the silo block. The silos began to topple and fell northward right onto a pile of soil that had been placed there to cushion the fall; thus, protecting the nearby houses from the shockwave as the giant structure fell to the ground. A large cloud of dust blew its way south and away from where we were standing. However, my mother and sister Stella were watching from Salt Lane, and soon found themselves amid a fog of cement dust. Later, I walked among the debris of the silos. The concrete shed that had been at the top of the silos was largely intact, and within that shed I found an industrial light. It was large and made of cream coloured enamelled steel of the type you'd expect to find in a pre-war factory; its big old light bulb had remained unbroken.

March 2nd 1980. This photograph is by courtessey of the Kent Messenger. Photograph copyright South Eastern Newspapers Ltd. Note the flock of pigeons flying away from the top of the silo.

Note in the above photograph the square structure at the very top of the silos and on the walkway just below it what appears to be a searchlight. These were possibly World War Two emplacements.

Silo block number 1. The set of 6 silos were demolished during 1980 with ball and chain. Photographs by Percy Payne.

CHAPTER 5

THE DAYS OF CHANGE

In 1981 some changes came to the landscape of Under the Hill in the form of a project to improve the sea defences. Over a 2-year period the level of the sea wall around Higham and Cliffe was raised. To enable the heavy lorries access to the sea wall, new roads were constructed: A fly-ash road was constructed over the County Wall track from Salt Lane across to Cliffe Creek. This new fly-ash road continued from the creek around the sea wall to Egypt Bay. And a new road made of aggregate was constructed over Black Lane, linking Salt Lane with the Point Road.

In constructing the new roadways, the old clay surface of the County Wall track and the flint and kiln cinder surface of Black Lane were erased and replaced with the imported material. Both roads were significantly widened in the process. Within a matter of days in 1981, that familiar and beloved old tunnel of hedgerows and trees which enveloped Black Lane were stripped away. In their wake came a wide road which soon became lined with by something I had not seen here hitherto: a profusion of buddleia soon established itself along the new road.

The sea wall project brought some changes to the Francis Chalk Quarry. A tall clay bund was constructed from the chalk hill to the foot of Percy's Hill, covering all of what remained of the old slurry backs and most of the northern part of Percy's Hill. In this time too, the wash mill was completely filled with soil.

The changes brought about in 1981 radically altered the character of the Track and Black Lane. Though today ghosts of the old Black Lane are still around: Parts of the original flint and cinder road can still be found in the undergrowth to the side of the new road: reminders of the industry that thrived along Black Lane a century ago. And the changes did not alter one iota our ventures Under the Hill.

Around the early 1980s Lower Hope Point was a place for days out and camping expeditions for a group of us: Alec Pennell, Robert Cox, Andrew Penniall and Paul Silver. We would set up our tents on the pastures around the old munitions works or camp along the sea wall with a driftwood fire to keep us warm. By night we would sit under the stars of the big dark sky over the marshes, watching the constellations gradually drift across the night sky. In the dark early hours, the vast constellation Orion in its strange frozen animation haunted the clear silent heavens above us.

Robert Cox really appreciated to the full the freedom our marshes provided. Robert was always jovial, always positive and cheerful, he is a great friend to be around. Andrew Cook would often join us too. Andrew became a good school friend of mine when he moved to Cliffe in the early 1970s. Andrew's father, known to us as Bill the Cowman, tended the cows on Cliffe marshes. Our days spent Under the Hill were full of laughs; these were happy and cheerful times of freedom. During our camping trips to the Point, we watched the progress of the sea wall construction and the changes it brought to our marshes. One change I remember well was of the old World War Two lookout post on the sea wall just west of the munitions works; it was of concrete construction and about ten feet in height. It was removed with the building of the new sea wall.

THE MARSHES BY AUTUMN'S LIGHT

Near to my 16th birthday I bought a Honda Benly for the Track; it was a 150 cc twin. I acquired an old crash helmet too: the matt white type with a fixed peak, just like police motorcyclists of old used to wear. It was a good bike for the track, but at 20 years it was starting to show its age and mileage. I took it for spin down the Track and descended the steep slippery Cliff Face. Even in the hottest summer months, Cliff Face always seemed to retain a sheen of moisture. I was mindful of my childhood escapade on the bicycle at Cliff Face: that hill could always spring a surprise. Some contemporaries of mine were in the Track, and my dated crash helmet caused some wry amusement.

What a wonderful sense of freedom that bike gave. The machine carried me along in magical flight. I could get from Pond Hill to Lower Hope Point in minutes! In the autumn of 1981 David Arnold and I took a ride out to Lower Hope Point; Arn rode pillion. I insisted that Arn wear the crash helmet, and he kind of hesitantly agreed. From Pond Hill to Lower Hope Point, we encountered not a sole; I suspect much to Arn's relief. During that mile or so journey we flew past luxuriant rain blessed meadows and bulrush beds that weaved the intricate story of the wind's every word. I proudly parked the bike outside of the brick hut that stood at the entrance gate to the munitions factory. Arn and I occupied the hut for the day like it was our own. We made a few excursions among the widely spaced ruins of the munitions works, returning to the hut when the odd squall shower blew our way.

The sky above our marsh was an endlessly fascinating myriad of puffy clouds racing in earnest across the clean blue. The marshes of our childhood had been as boundless as our imaginations could take us. As teenagers that vastness hadn't diminished, and on this day its full splendour lay before us like never before. There was a dynamic aspect to the landscape on that day. The marsh was transformed into a canvas upon which the sky expressed its every change of character, it's every shift of mood, with tones painted by brilliant shafts of sunlight between shadows of the darkest rain soaked grey.

Afternoon brought hunger; it was time to return home. The motorbike sprang into life at the first kick – only to die the moment we tried to move off. After a half hour of tinkering with HT leads and fuel pipes, bump starting and false hopes, we resigned to the inevitable. It was a long walk home, taking it in turns to push the sluggish dead weight of the bike. But beyond the ambience of that day, nothing seemed to bother us too much.

Back home I got to work immediately on the bike, stripping the carb and cleaning spark plugs until it was too dark to see. And the next day at the bottom of Pond Hill the bike sprang to life, full of promise. It took me all the way to Lower Hope Point again. I took a walk among the mudflats, looking for clay pipes and pointed Hamilton bottles of Tubby Slater's time. All the time, the bike stood poised upon the sea wall proudly upright upon its centre stand. But no ride home: the bike again refused to start. It was a long push back without Arn to help.

By now my enthusiasm for motorbikes had run its course. Ken Arnold at the old bakery house just across the street from us had a friend who could foresee the potential of this vintage bike. I got a good price for the Benly.

THE BICYCLE MAN

The same year my parents bought for me a new 10 gear racing bicycle, a form of transport more in tune with the lifestyle of a man who in my teenage years became a role model for me: my old friend Herbert Weber. Herbert and I shared a common affinity for the outdoors, and I think Herbert spent as much time Under the Hill as he did in his flat in Newberry Close Cliffe Woods. Swimming was Herbert's forte, and true to character his swimming habits were unique and unconventional. He swam always fully clothed, and swimming fully clothed didn't hinder his swimming: he always swam in a slow unhurried breast stroke and never too far from the bank. One time Herbert found a railway sleeper washed up on the banks of the creek which he dragged all the way to the Crystal Lake. "The log" as he always referred to it became his swimming aid at the Crystal for many years, greatly extending the range of his leisurely swims. Many a Sunday morning I would cycle along the old Francis tramway to the Crystal, and my first sight of the Crystal would be of Herbert floating free in the water. With the little log completely submerged under his weight, Herbert resembled an otter in its element - Herbert looked completely at home out there in the water.

On an old gate post down in the meadow by the bank of the old Francis tramway Herbert would lean his bicycle. When Herbert camped overnight as he sometimes did, a low green tent would be nestled among the tall straw like grass of the meadow. The tent looked as natural in that meadow as the button mushrooms Herbert liked to pick in autumn. After his swim, Herbert hung his denim jacket on a hawthorn bush to dry in the sun. He kept his wet shirt, trousers and shoes on all day; he never seemed uncomfortable in this squelching attire. Sunbathing in the summer sun, Herbert engaged in his great curiosity for words by completing newspaper crosswords. He spent his afternoons analysing the cryptic crosswords of his newspaper and fully completing them. A famous part of Herbert's outdoor kit was his transistor radio on which he listened to two channels. Of a Saturday afternoon Herbert would listen to Radio 4's just a minute, both amused and amazed by the linguistic antics of Kenneth Williams and company. BBC World Service was the other channel Herbert listened to. The quaint tones of the World Service news hour signature tune seemed fitting to Herbert. Herbert's sustenance for the day would be kept in his sun faded canvas saddlebag: usually a sweet pastry and a single small can of beer, and only ever a branded German beer. Sometimes he would bring along an old glass lemonade bottle into which he had squeezed the juice several lemons and added sugar and water.

On the banks of the Crystal Herbert would sometimes reminisce of the dark days of the regime that had led his country to war, of his days as a prisoner of war in America, and of his early years, adventurous and happy years, in his adopted country. Herbert came to the Hoo peninsula in 1966 when the bomb disposal unit for which he worked relocated from Horsham to Chattenden. Knowing Herbert's love of the outdoors, a colleague had recommended Cliffe Creek, and the area was to become Herbert's second home for 21 years. Herbert came to Cliffe Marshes when the Alpha was still in operation, and he recalled some scenes of that time. On a still summer's day in the late 1960s, the smoke from the Alpha chimneys rose in straight columns and perfectly reflected on the still waters of the Crystal; a real picture indeed. Herbert spent long weekend days at the creek then rode home along the County Wall of an evening. As darkness fell, the only light upon the marsh was a lamp shining from the pontoon crane out on the Crystal Lake.

Herbert had experienced first-hand in his life the ravaged history that came to shape our modern world. And just like Dunkirk and Burma veteran Uncle Eddie, he was a man who projected great patience and forbearing born of great modesty and a stoic contentment with his post-war life. The life that Herbert found among the clay lakes of our marshes was indeed one of contentment.

Indeed, in his calm contentment Herbert was the embodiment of the tranquil life. There seemed only to be one thing that ever brought him close to anger: the egg collectors who came from afar to raid the bird nests of the islands of the Crystal and of Swan Lake. When the egg collectors came, Herbert would wave his arms in the air and shout across the lake "Leave them alone! Leave them alone!". This would send the egg collectors running. Egg collectors, who collected bird's eggs for display purposes were a big problem in the 1970s and 1980s that bothered us locals greatly. When they came to the clay lakes, some of the local lads who swam with Herbert would run up to the village to call the local policeman, then the egg collectors felt he force of the law. There is a string of islands that span Swan Lake from the east to the west. At the eastern end, only a very shallow stretch of water isolated the islands from the mainland. In fact, this was often a dry land bridge when the water level in the lakes was low. Over this narrow land bridge, the egg collectors gained access to the islands. Herbert had a pro-active approach to the problem. One day he came to Swan Lake with a shovel strapped to his bicycle. He dug a deep and wide trench across that land bridge, hence protecting the nests of the many swans and gulls that nested on the islands. The swans of the lakes came to know Herbert well. Herbert would bring along in his saddlebag old bread to which he fed the swans who would take the bread directly from Herbert's hand.

As Herbert sat as he often did, gazing out upon the lakes, I often wondered what thoughts lay behind those grey eyes. In conversation he would oftentimes ponder the roots of words; words used in our everyday language that most of us never gave a second thought to. A kilometre across the marsh from the Crystal sat the huge sand hills of the Marinex gravel works, and Herbert one day wondered from where the acronym Marinex was derived. "Marine Excavation" was his analysis: That makes sense: the sand and gravel of the Marinex plant are excavated from the sea bed.

One time Herbert posed to me the question while pointing to an elder blossom: *"How does the plant know how to grow in such a reproducible and precise form, and how does it know where to grow the leaves and that the leaves are to be green, and that at a certain time of year the blossom comes and it is to be coloured white?"* I gave some explanation about genes, chlorophyll and pigments. My answer drew a blank look from Herbert: I sensed that my explanation had hardly touched the surface of the deeper question that Herbert was really pondering. Those were the thoughts of a man who was most at home among the rough grass and the bramble bushes of the Crystal.

Come harvest time, Herbert's saddle bag would be filled with boxes of blackberries picked from the brambles that grew along the path to the Crystal. Back in his flat Herbert would make blackberry jam, and from sloes picked from the bushes of Creek Road he would make sloe gin. I sometimes make sloe gin from sloes of the very same trees. To this day the smell of sloe gin takes me straight back to the early 1980s and Herbert's tidy flat where we toasted Christmas eve with shot glasses of sloe gin - never more than a thimble full mind. New Year's Eve brought more festivities - Herbert style. We would board the train at Higham and celebrate the turn of the year with the thousands of other revellers splashing around in the fountain pools of Trafalgar Square as midnight chimed from Big Ben. On one such occasion as we danced in the icy water, a young woman from the multitude gave Herbert a big hug with the words "Well done granddad!" I was as surprised as was Herbert: Granddad? I only ever saw Herbert as a youth, an eternal youth, just like the rest of us.

Over the Christmas holiday Herbert would visit our family. Ever respectful in the tradition of his time, he only addressed my parents as Mr Tester and Mrs Tester, even though my parents preferred he used first names. From his saddle bag he produced his projector and photo slides of his travels to the wild lands of Wales. In my teenage years I accompanied Herbert on many a camping holiday in Wales. By virtue of Herbert I experienced the grand tranquillity of Snowdon and Cadair Idris. We would take our bikes across the Plynlimon mountain range within an area known as the green desert of Wales. Amid this wonderfully isolated land we would stop by a stream to camp and cook our meals. In the far distance we might see some tiny figures on a far ridge: the only sight of people we might have in days. I emulated Herbert in his simple lifestyle embodied in his simple diet. We took water from the streams to cook pasta to which we added spam crudely cut into chunks. Bread was an essential part of the diet; for Herbert only white uncut in crusty bloomer loaves. Herbert ate bread with salami sausage onto which he placed sliced raw chillies. He ate apples held firmly in his hand as he bit with his lower jaw: his upper front teeth had long gone due to calcium deficiency in his childhood a dentist once told him. Though in his whole life, Herbert would never succumb to dentures. Naturally Herbert became acquainted with the Welsh language. Most of the words he knew were those which he reasoned from the maps he had: Llyn for lake etc. When I travel in Wales today, those place names take me back to those times, and in my mind those welsh place names come to me in a distinctly German accent. In those places my eyes were opened to the grandeur of the wider world beyond Cliffe, places I would never had known but for my friendship with this unique man whom I had first met as a toddler along with my brothers and sisters among the salt marshes of Cliffe Creek.

1985 brought retirement for Herbert. His colleagues at Chattenden Army Camp bought a brand-new bicycle as his retirement present. With so much free time on his hands he spent every summer's day Under the Hill. By the mid 1980s the waters of the Crystal had changed: the waters of the clay lakes had become cloudy and clogged in places with weed. This was something that had affected the Wellcome yacht club causing it to close. Hence, we changed our swimming venue to Cliffe Creek.

Sometimes we would ride our bicycles along the sea wall path from Cliffe Creek to Egypt Bay for a swim in its shallow warm summer waters. We would pass the Point Beacon at the Waterman's Stone at Lower Hope Point. The beacon was a slender iron tower as high as a house. It had a cube structure at the top, but no light. As we progressed toward Egypt Bay, the Point Beacon shrank to the distance until it became a remote enigma in the landscape. We took our bikes further afield too: on the train from Higham to Rye and camped out along the lonely shingle beach at Lydd Range.

Herbert and I swimming in Cliffe Creek in September 1985.

Herbert faced something of a dilemma after his retirement. He was entitled to a German state pension based on contributions he had made from his earnings before and during the war. But in order to qualify for the pension he was required to live in Germany. Certainly, he felt settled in England; he had indeed been awarded dual

British/German citizenship around 1970 at the time he had taken a civil service exam. After a couple of years' consideration Herbert decided to move to Germany. In February 1987 he moved to a flat in Duisburg close to his nephew. It was a big wrench for Herbert, and he visited us in England at least once a year. He was happy in Duisburg living close to his family. I visited him a number of times which gave me the opportunity to see this quiet German town and also the magnificent city of Koln nearby. In fact, on the banks of the river Rhine not far from his flat, Herbert found a swimming spot amid a band of salt marsh in appearance much like Cliffe Creek. And in Herbert's later years, he began to attend a local church in Duisburg. "What they say makes sense to me" Herbert told me. I believe that there, Herbert found the answer to his question about the elder blossom.

THE END OF A GREAT LANDMARK OF OUR MARSHES

The 1980s brought a change too for another good friend of mine, Aunt Sis. In 1985 Aunt Sis moved from her home at Quarry Cottages. It was the year of her 84th birthday and she had decided that she needed to live closer to the village. Although she was sad to leave Quarry Cottages, Aunt Sis was happy closer to her family in her new home with its modern facilities at Pond Hill. Within a day of her moving, her old home was demolished. It was something that she had been expecting. In the years leading up to her moving she had often joked to me that I ought to squat in Quarry Cottages after she left in order to prevent their demolition. I remember walking among the rubble of Quarry Cottages on that poignant day in 1985. I took a piece of the horse hair and lime plaster from the rubble as a keepsake of this house that had been a landmark of Under the Hill for many generations. Aunt Sis spent comfortable years close to her family at Pond Hill. She passed away in 1992 in her 91st year.

But the end of Quarry Cottages was not the end of habitation Under the Hill. One family, Collins, who had moved from London in the 1960s, continued to live in the Coastguard Cottages until a time close their demolition in 1994. And for a few years in the late 1980s Cliffe Creek was host to a number of house boats. The folks of the Cliffe Creek house boats would collect their mail from my mother at the post office. One couple were artists and gave my mother one of their paintings.

After Mr and Mrs Baxter moved up to the village, Boatwick House became the home of Trevor and Jacqueline Morrison and their children Patrick, Sarah and Kerry from around 1980/1 to 1987/88. Today, Ken and Carol Baxter live in the old family home Boatwick House and farm sheep on the marshes just as in Jack Baxter's days.

THE BIG CLEAN UP

In the late 1980s, a tragedy began to beset Under the Hill: fly-tipping. Old car tires, broken windscreens, fridges and all manner of commercial waste were brought from afar and illegally dumped. The picnic grounds had become a shadow of what we had known hitherto. Where had once been green grass was now a mass of broken glass, plastic and builder's rubble. This concerned the people of Cliffe greatly, and in the early 1990s someone in Cliffe organised a mass clear up of the rubbish that blighted Pickles Way, Black Lane and Creek Road. Organised and implemented by local people, the turnout was huge: they came with black bin liners, gathering rubbish from under every bush. Several skip loads of rubbish were collected and taken away.

THE SEA WALL FOOTPATH RS357

The sea wall footpath from Cliffe Creek to Egypt Bay had for generations been an established footpath, though as of the late 1980s the sea wall footpath was not marked as a right of way on the definitive map. In 1989 I started a campaign to get the sea wall footpath classified as a right of way. I needed a name for this campaign, and my father came up with: *The Hoo Peninsula Footpath Amenities Campaign*. My father produced a letter head from commercially available sheets of transferable typefaces:

The Hoo Peninsula Footpath Amenities Campaign

Our footpath campaign letter head produced by Victor Tester Senior.

I put together petition forms which people could sign with the number of years that they had walked the path, and my parents and I put the petition forms in our shop for people to sign. We had an overwhelming response from Cliffe people and from people who came to Cliffe to enjoy our marshes: over 300 signatures in all. Kent County Council were very supportive, and on 4th March 1991 they confirmed the public right of way from Cliffe Creek to Egypt Bay High Halstow, and the footpath was named RS357. This was a great team effort to secure a public right of way around our marshes for all the people to enjoy and for future generations, long may it remain.

Our footpath campaign comes to fruition on a sunny spring day in 1991 with Council notices confirming the right of way around our sea wall. Thanks to my mum and dad, to all who signed our petition, and to Kent County Council. Photograph by Clive Tester.

EPILOGUE: THE VIEW FROM THE 21ST CENTURY.

In October of 2001, Herbert made the journey from Germany to visit our family in Cliffe. As he had done so often in the past, he came with bags bulging with gifts for friends and erstwhile colleagues. He brought to us things of his country, things which we loved to receive: packets of potato dumplings called knodel, smoked eel, jars of German caviar and liqueurs. Likewise, in Herbert's years in England, he had often made the journey to Germany visiting his family and bearing in the same kindly manner bags bulging with gifts. While we waved goodbye as he boarded his coach at Farthing Corner, we were not to know that this would be Herbert's last visit. Herbert passed away unexpectedly on May 28th 2002. Like George Herbert Burton, Herbert in his eternal youth embodied the spirit of innocent playful freedom of the places that we all knew Under the Hill.

In the summer of that same year I took a walk to the Crystal. The old gatepost on which Herbert once leaned his bicycle was hidden by an encroaching thicket of elder, hawthorn and bramble: the deeper nature of those plants Herbert had once pondered by the banks of the Crystal. And the waters of the Crystal were quiet, for the clay lakes had long before ceased to be a place for swimming. The only sound at the Crystal that day was of the cool wind in the old hawthorn trees where we long ago hung our clothes to dry. At the Crystal, our playful shouts and splashing were of yesteryear.

Today, nature is in the ascendant Under the Hill. At Creek Road a tall reed bed flourishes around the area where the old Ivy House once stood. And upon the muddy flats of the creek where the salt marsh long ago diminished in the wake of industry, silt has settled upon which spartina grass now grows. Perhaps in a century from now, the creek will resemble its pre-industrial days as the old salt marsh returns.

In the first year of the 21st century the clay lakes came under the remit of the Royal Society for the Protection of Birds, and hence Under the Hill has changed in its role. It is a change that can be viewed as part of the evolution of Under the Hill in the past 100 years, from a place of industry, to a place for leisure activities and finally a wildlife sanctuary managed in the name of conservation and sustainability. It is a change that will meet the pressures on our local countryside that the new century brings.

Under the Hill in the protection of its new custodians will continue to be a place to find solitude and reflection, a place that will always have character and always have great value. Under the Hill should provide for the local young people of future generations a place to engage in conservation in action. For our picnic grounds and our clay lakes will always be a place that belongs in spirit to the local folk who valued in so many different ways their marshes, and to those who will in the future continue to do so: the children from Monkey Island, past present and future.

Clive Tester December 2015

APPENDIX A

THE LIME KILN OF PICKLE'S WAY

Close to a small chalk quarry at Pickle's Way Cliffe, lies a lime kiln hidden in the woods. Around the 1930s, a man called Bill Topley lived in the lime kiln for many years[i]. Bill was from a "well to do family" of Cliffe[ii].

In 1982 the lime kiln was excavated by the Lower Medway Archaeological Group[iii], and this was initiated by Percy Payne of Strood after the kiln had been shown to him by Clive Tester[iv]. The lime kiln was dated to the mid-19th century and was probably constructed by a local farmer to provide agricultural lime[iii].

Two photographs of the Pickle's Way lime kiln taken shortly after its excavation. A close examination of the inner surface of the kiln revealed a surface resembling melted black glass, consisting of many droplets and runs of solidified silica that had been heated to melting point when the kiln was in operation[iv]. Photographs by Clive Tester 1982.

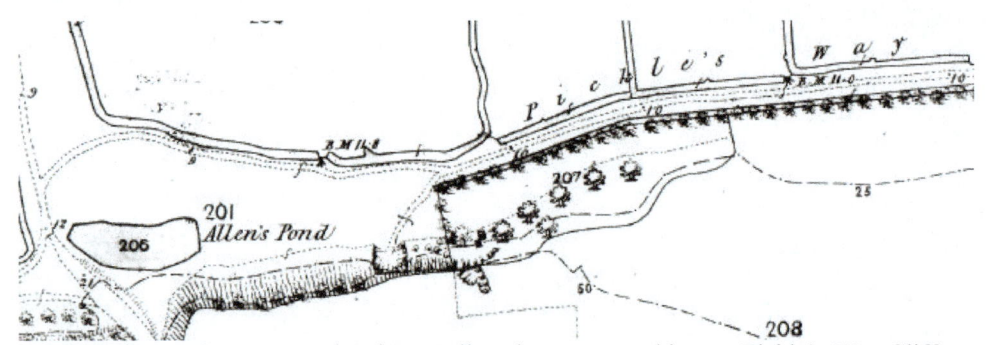

1860 Ordnance Survey map showing small-scale quarry workings at Pickle's Way Cliffe.

CITATIONS FOR APPENDIX A

i: Gwen Tester.
ii: Mildred Hoare AKA Aunt Sis.
iii: The Hoo Peninsula. Philip MacDougall. John Hallewell Publications 1980. ISBN 0 905540 19 0.
iv: Clive Tester.

APPENDIX B:

LAYER, PELDON AND THE ALPHA RAILWAYS.

INTRODUCTION

Among a fleet of fifteen industrial diesel locomotives, which operated at the Alpha Cement Factory at Salt Lane Cliffe, Peldon was one of three Fowler diesel locomotives which ran in the factory's chalk pits.

Technical details for Peldon, John Fowler Resilient Class No. 21295/1936: -
- **Manufacturer:** John Fowler & Co. (Leeds) Ltd.
- **Date of manufacture:** 1936
- **Gauge:** 2 ft
- **Power Output:** 40 horsepower
- **Engine:** Fowler Sanders 4 cyl engine No. M443 B series.

HISTORY

Construction of the Abberton Reservoir near Colchester in Essex began in 1935, and three Fowler Resilient 40 horsepower diesel engines were ordered for the project. These were delivered in April 1936. The engines were named after villages, which surrounded the 4.25 by 1.5mile long reservoir; these were Abberton No.21293, Peldon No. 21295 and Layer No.21294 named after the village Layer–De-La-Haye. A fourth engine, Romford No. 21408 named after the water company's head office, was delivered in October 1936. Following the completion of the Abberton Reservoir in 1939 the four engines were sold; Romford was with Blue Circle Cement in the Hastings area by 1939[*]. Stan Beeching recalled for this book that Peldon, Abberton and Layer went to the Alpha Cement Company at Cliffe in 1939.

Fowler engine Peldon in the third Alpha Pit in 1969 or 1970. Photograph courtesy of David Willis.

Stan Beeching recalled that the three Fowler locomotives were bought with the intention of them being used on the railway system within the cement factory and on the railway line that linked the cement factory with the jetty. However, it was found that the Fowler engines were incompatible height wise with some of the overhead equipment on those lines. So instead, the three Fowler engines were used in the chalk quarries of Salt Lane. Stan recalled that, of the late 1930s, there were three narrow gauge railway systems operating at the Alpha, but these three lines were not linked. The three lines, totalling approximately 1.5 miles, were: -

- From the chalk quarry excavator to terminate at the wash mills that resided in the chalk quarry to the south of the factory. At the wash mills, flints were separated from the chalk (see the map on page 161). The Fowler locomotives pulled three or four high framed wooden wagons; each wagon could carry three to four tons of chalk. Allen Tipton wagons were also used.
- From the wash mills, flints were sent on another railway line a short distance due west to a haulage point that also resided in the quarry. At this location, the flints were hauled out of the quarry to the factory by a mechanism that had been in place since the Thames Portland Cement era (This mechanism had originally been used to take chalk from the quarry back when Thames Portland Cement owned the factory in the period up to 1934). Once hauled out of the quarry, the flints were transported by rail on the factory line that took it under the raised coal railway line and to the north side of the factory where the stone plant resided beside the factory stores (see the maps on pages 160 and 162).
- A narrow-gauge line ran within the factory. The line also linked the cement packing plant and the coal handling plant with the jetty a mile to the north where cement was despatched by ship and coke was delivered for the factory. Ruston and Hornsby diesel locomotives were used on this 2 ft narrow gauge railway system.

By the late 1950s the narrow-gauge fleet of fifteen diesel locomotives was in need of repair, and due to the lack of available spare parts some were cannibalised to keep others working. From that period, the diesel fleet was used only sporadically, and the fleet was eventually abandoned.

Stan Beeching recalled that during the 1960s, the railway system within the quarries was replaced with dumper trucks. The railway lines in the quarry tunnels were replaced with concrete roads. Stan Beeching laid the flints on the tunnel roadways onto which the concrete was laid. Some modifications to the wash mill tipping arrangement were required due to the change from locomotives to dumper trucks.

Peldon. Photograph by Gordon Edgar 24th January 1971. Third Alpha Pit.

David Willis with a Fowler engine in the third Alpha Pit in 1969 or 1970. Photograph courtesy of David Willis.

Fowler engine Peldon in the third Alpha Pit in 1969 or 1970. Photograph courtesy of David Willis.

Ruston &Hornsby locomotives on the line from the wash mills to the haulage point. Photograph by Gordon Edgar 24th January 1971.

Peldon (foreground) with Layer (background). Photograph by Gordon Edgar 24th January 1971.
Third Alpha Pit.

Layer. Photograph by Gordon Edgar 24th January 1971.
Third Alpha Pit.

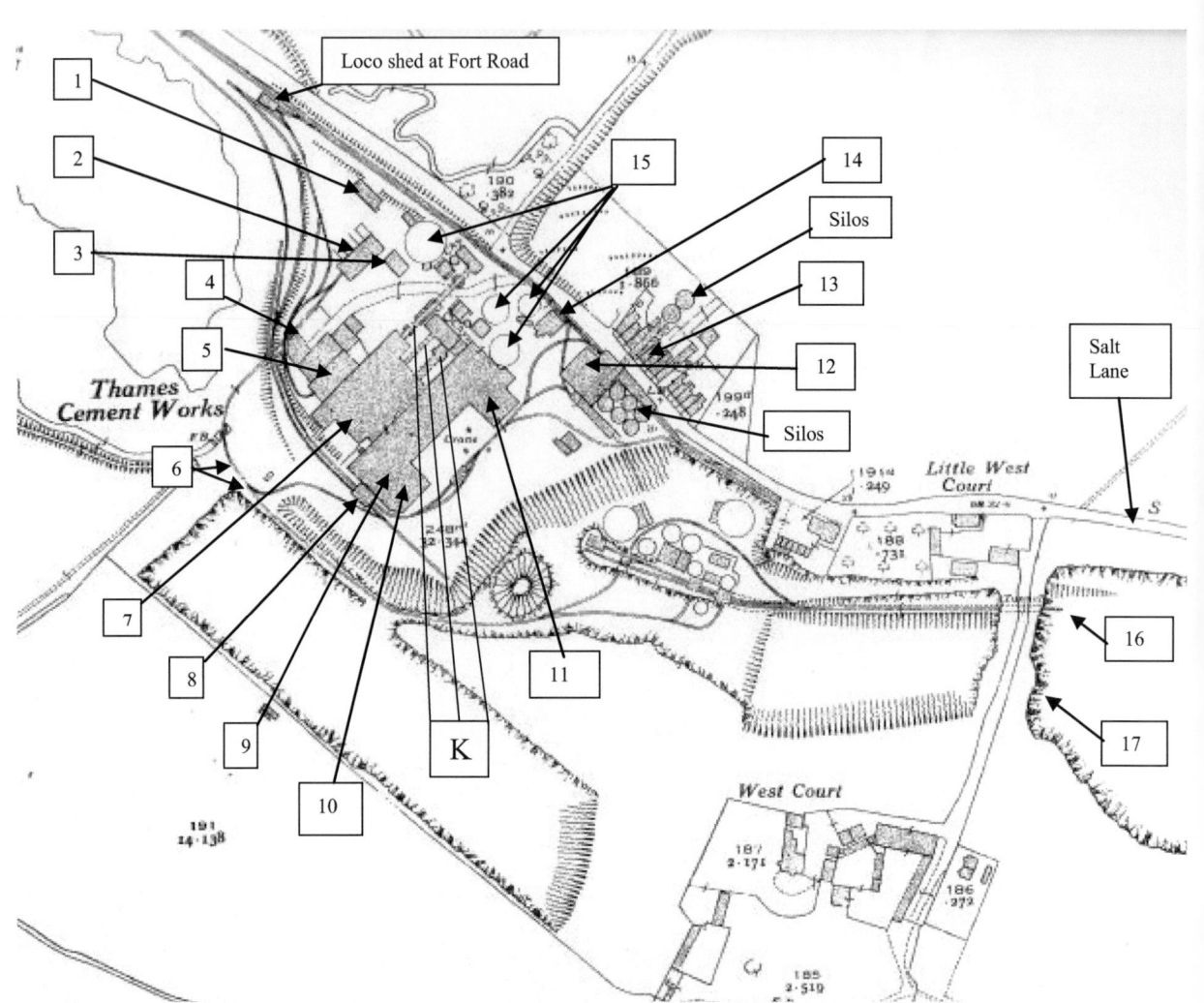

The railway lines and the essential elements of the Alpha. The annotations on the map and the key below are from information provided by Stan Beeching. Reproduced from the 1939 Ordnance Survey map.

Key: -

1: Wash room and toilets.
2: Fitting shop.
3: Canteen.
4: Stone plant. The road marked on the map ran from the stone plant to a location near to the points 14 and 15 on the map where a weigh bridge was located. Here the trucks loaded with stones bound for the Staffordshire potteries were weighed.
5: Store for bulk items.
6: Stone railway.
7: Kiln platform
8: Coal tip (attached to the Clinker Shed). The coal railway ran from the north over a raised ramp under which the stone railway line passed.
9: Coal store.
10: In the appendage was the grinding media store (steel balls of various sizes and 1-inch diameter steel rods cut into approximately 1 inch sections, to act as grinding media).
11: From right to left, grinding mills 1, 2 and 3.
12: Packing plants.
13: The row of houses at Salt Lane including the Royal Albert Pub and Concrete Cottages.
14: Laboratory.
15: Slurry basins.
16: The 25-foot drop tunnel.
17: In this period though not marked on the map, a deeper tunnel ran from this point.
K: From bottom to top of the map, kilns 1,2 and 3.

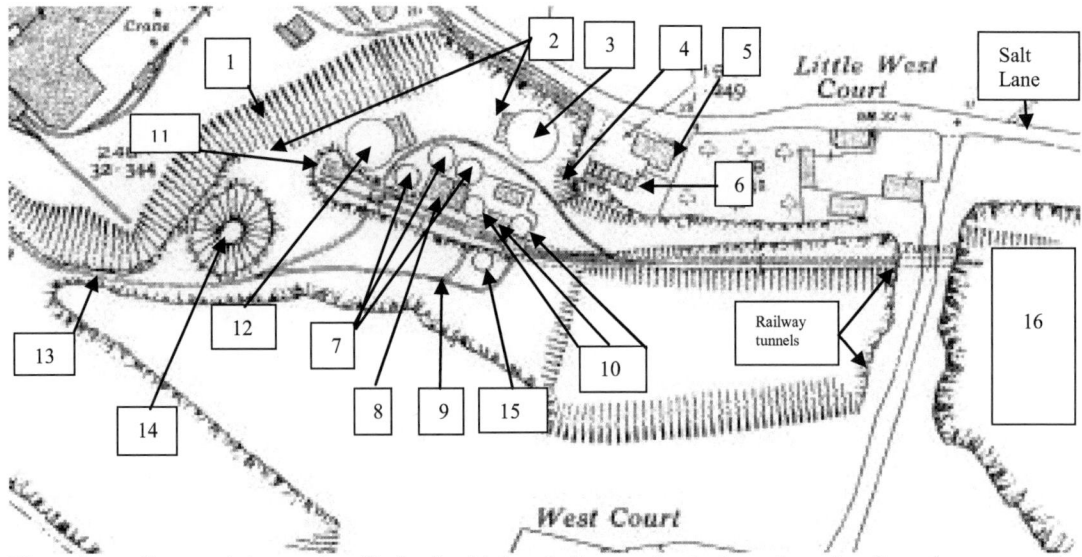

The railway lines and the wash mills in the Alpha chalk quarries (enlarged section from the map on the previous page). The annotations on the map and the key below are from a map that was drawn by Stan Beeching in 2016 especially for this book. Reproduced from the 1939 Ordnance Survey map.

Key: -

1: Access steps into the quarry.
2: Between the arrows ran a pipeline through which clay was pumped from the pontoon cranes on Cliffe marshes via a booster pump located at Fort Road.
3: Clay basin for storage of clay into which the clay pipeline (see 2 above) ran.
4: Mess room.
5: Former home with a garden of the Thames Portland Cement Manager pre-1932. Later this became the Alpha/APCM offices with a documentation store located in the cellar of the building.
6: Garages. The first garage in the row was for the works car.
7: Slurry mixer basins.
8: Wash mill house containing slurry refining apparatus, i.e. tubular grinding mill, Trix mills, etc.
9: Stone railway.
10: From left to right: Wash mill number 1/ Wash mill motor house/ Wash mill number 2.
11: Loco repair shed.
12: Prepared slurry basin.
13: The Ramp: this was a steep incline out of the quarry which was too steep for the locomotives to haul stone laden trucks. This area is the haulage point mentioned on page 156, where the stone trucks were decoupled from the quarry locomotives and hauled over rails up the steep incline by a wire cable winch system. At the top of the incline, the stone trucks were coupled with locomotives that ran to the stone plant.
14: This was a small hill of chalk upon which many flints that were taken from the top soil of the quarry had been placed during the Thames Portland Cement era. The flint mound was very popular with bird watchers because wagtails used to nest within the flints.
15: Stone wash out.
16: Location of the Fowler engines and trucks shown in the photographs on pages 84 and 155 to 159.

Slurry process flow: Chalk was tipped from the railway trucks into the chalk "tips" located at the southern side of the circular wash mills at location 10 in the map above. At this point clay that was pumped from point 3 was blended with the chalk, and the flints were separated from the chalk and the flints sent away via the stone railway. Unrefined slurry ran via a slurry trough to the wash mill house at point 8 where upon it was further refined. The slurry was finished at point 12 on the map. The finished slurry was pumped via a pipeline to the factory.

Little West Court: Stan Beeching recalls that this was once a farm with a thatched cottage. From this farm, the field that is now the chalk pit to the east of the road to West Court Farm was ploughed for crops. Mr Day was the ploughman of Little West Court.

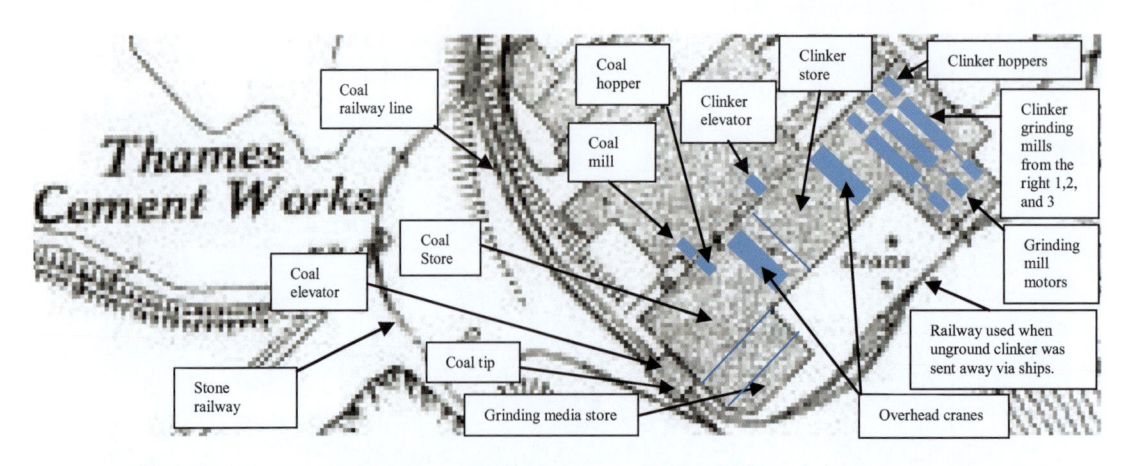

The elements of the Clinker Shed and associated railways. The annotations on the map are from a map that was drawn by Stan Beeching in 2016 especially for this book. Reproduced from the 1939 Ordnance Survey map with additions for this book added in blue.

RESTORATION

Brockham Museum Association volunteer Gordon Edgar visited the Alpha pits on 24th January 1971. At this time, Layer and Peldon lay rusting whilst Abberton had been removed. Gordon was instrumental in making Pete Nicholson and Dave Billmore of the Brockham Museum Association aware of the survival of the John Fowler locomotives. Arrangements were made with the owners for the purchase of the engines. The Brockham Museum Association performed the removal of the engines from the pits. In July 1972 Peldon and Layer arrived at Brockham.

Both locomotives were in a very poor condition and in December 1974 it was decided to strip both locomotives of their parts to ascertain which was in the better condition. It was found that Peldon was in the better shape for restoration, and Layer was therefore sent to another railway group. Layer is currently in storage at Armley Mills Leeds Industrial Museum.

Douglas F Bentley started restoration work in 1978. Because the locomotive had been abandoned for so many years, restoration was a time-consuming task which required considerable dedication and technical expertise. The restorers had to contend with among other problems, ceased parts, a cracked piston and worn or missing parts. Upon opening the crank case doors of the large four-cylinder engine, oil sludge and water flooded out. The engine had been half full due to the accumulation of rain and condensation over the years. The fuel tank had rusted badly, and inside was discovered an abandoned field mouse nest. Extensive work was also required on the main frames the bodywork and the cab.

The restored train ran for the first time in June 1987, and restoration work was completed on the 3rd of July 1988. Today, Peldon can be seen in operation pulling passenger wagons at the Amberley Museum & Heritage Centre in West Sussex.

An in-depth account of the history and restoration of Peldon is available in the form of a booklet *The Story of Peldon* by Douglas F Bentley and can be obtained from the Amberley Museum & Heritage Centre, cited below.

Peldon at Cliffe in 1972, and Peldon after restoration at Amberley. Images courtesy of the Amberley Museum & Heritage Centre.

ACKNOWLEDGMENTS FOR APPENDIX B

A special thanks is extended to Stan Beeching for information provided and for the detailed maps that he prepared for this book.

A special thanks is extended to the Amberley Museum & Heritage Centre for the information and images of Peldon so graciously provided.

A special thanks is extended to David Willis for his information regarding the locomotives of the Alpha pits and photographs of Layer and Peldon from his visit to the Alpha pits in 1969/1970.

A special thanks is extended to Gordon Edgar for providing photographs from his visit to the Alpha pits in 1971 and to Tony Millatt of the Mersea Museum for helping with my enquiries.

This appendix was prepared using the following information sources: -

Amberley Museum & Heritage Centre
Houghton Bridge
Amberley
Arundel
West Sussex. BN18 9LT.
Tel. 01798 831 370. Web site www.amberleymuseum.co.uk

The Story of Peldon by Douglas F Bentley, 1989. Available at the Amberley Museum & Heritage Centre. (Citation from which is marked with * on page155).

Stan Beeching, chalk quarry excavator operator, chalk quarry foreman and shift production foreman at the Alpha Cliffe.

Armley Mills. Leeds Industrial Museum. www.leeds.gov.uk/armleymills/

The Cement Railways of Kent by B.D. Stoyel and R.W. Kidner, 1990, ISBN 0 85361 370 2.

The Isle of Grain Railways by Adrian Gray. The Oakwood Press 1974. Locomotion papers number 77.

APPENDIX C

"HAM, SPAM OR JAM"

MEMORIES OF THE ALPHA

There was a character to old industrial Cliffe embodied in the skyline to the west where towering chimneys and cavernous cement silos lay swathed within a wonderfully curious latticework of conveyor belts pipes and iron gantries. Back in the day, columns of white steamy smoke ascended forth into the sky from the chimneys of the cement works known locally as the Alpha. It was a dusty kind of smoke: cement manufacture is a dusty business. Oftentimes cement powder settled over Cliffe dusting windows roofs and washing alike.

It was a time when Cliffe folk didn't need cars to drive out of the village for work. Each day employees of the cement works rode to work on bicycles. And those days are remembered with fondness by the Cliffe families who once earned their living from the Alpha. People like Terry Hoare whose father Basil worked in the Salt Lane chalk quarries alongside Reg Pennell, Sid Wheeler and Quarry Foreman Stan Beeching. Of a night time, Terry recalled, a big searchlight on the edge of the cliff at Salt Lane shone down into the depths of the chalk pit to guide the men working on the excavator. Of an evening when his dad worked a late shift Terry used to deliver his dinner to the mess hut deep in the quarry near to West Court Farm.

The chalk quarry mess hut in 1959. The man in the chequered shirt is Basil Hoare who drove the RB54 chalk excavator. The man in the right foreground is Sid Wheeler.
Photograph courtesy of Terry Hoare.

A sense of community around the cement works existed in that time. As children in the 1950s, Terry Hoare and his friends oftentimes walked to a cricket pitch that once lay to the south west of the Alpha near to where the Brett gravel works stands today. They approached from Salt Lane and walked right through the cement factory. Their route took them under the rotary kilns where the heat was intense and the noise deafening as those revolving furnaces roared with the inferno that they contained. Onto the quietness of the marshes beyond the cement works their route took them past a stream of clear water pumped day and night from the chalk quarry onto the marsh. Folk used to collect an abundance of elvers from that man-made stream.

Big and genial Perce Springhall, a man always happy to lend a hand, worked in the cement works' "Heavy Gang" who specialised in heavy manual labour and he helped to dig the quarry railway tunnel under Salt Lane. As a child in the 1950s and 1960s Perce's son Terry oftentimes visited the place of his father's work and like Terry Hoare walked amid the factory and under the hot rotary kilns. An abundance of coal abound at the cement works as Terry Springhall recalls. On winter days and nights coal stoves blazed away the cold within the multitude of corrugated iron sheds and creosoted wooden buildings of the Alpha. And it was on one such snowy winter's day when the coal fires burned that Stan Beeching recalled a close call. Dining in the Alpha canteen he and his workmates heard the sound of metal grinding against metal from the direction of the Clinker Shed as its vast corrugated iron roof groaned under the weight of the fallen snow. It collapsed but thankfully no one was hurt.

At lunch times in the Alpha canteen, Perce Springhall always had cheese rolls made by Milli "Aunt Sis" Hoare. Paul Scott reflected on that time: "Remember Aunt Sis she worked in the canteen when I was apprentice at the cement works in the mid-sixties… bless her she was a character and loved by everyone. Some of the guys tried winding her up but she gave as good as she got. They used to say what sandwiches you got today Sis?…she answered Ham, Spam or Jam. Happy days".

Aunt Sis' home at Quarry Cottages lay amid the clay lakes upon which her husband Bert worked. Bert along with Eric Slater, Dick Dowsett and others from Cliffe operated the pontoon cranes that worked the marshes expanding the area of the clay lakes each day to supply clay to the Alpha and the cement works at Swanscombe. Eric Slater recalled that they always took care to dig around areas where they saw birds nesting so as not to disturb the nest. The clay lakes today have many little islands.

Cliffe Marshes formed part of a wider Cliffe community encompassing the two homes of Quarry Cottages, Ivy House at Creek Road, the Coast Guard Cottages and also houses at Cliffe Creek. In the 1950s Terry Hoare often visited the Madden family in their bungalow at the mouth of Cliffe Creek. Its garden presented a luxuriant scene with a bright flowery rose arch standing at the porch of the bungalow. Terry Hoare recalled of that time: My brother and I spent many a very happy time there playing with Tommy the son and Rosy his younger sister. Brian and I obtained our two pigeons from Tommy and we subsequently bred and kept more of these over the years. Mrs. Madden was a lovely lady who always welcomed us into her house and I still remember [some forty years later] being very saddened on hearing of her death. I can still hear her voice, even today.

The bungalow at Cliffe Creek where the Madden family lived. When Terry and Brian Hoare oftentimes visited in the 1950s the house presented an idyllic picture with a large climbing rose bush around the porch area in the foreground and flower beds in the garden. Photograph courtesy of Catherine Groves.

Over yonder across the marshes come the end of the shift a siren sounded at the Alpha to be heard all the way to the quarries. Shortly after, dozens of folks on cement covered bicycles rode home along Salt Lane. And as was the way at the time all took the junction at Norward Corner without stopping and leaning as they took the turn as if in some big bicycle race. But one day back in the 1950s, Terry Springhall recalls, the local policeman waited by Norward Corner: he booked every one of the dozens of cyclists for not stopping at the junction. Even the earnest and obliging Perce Springhall of the Alpha's Heavy Gang received a fine.

APPENDIX D.

A SWALLOW FALLS OVER EGYPT BAY

THE DE HAVILLAND DH108 SWALLOW AIR CRASH

On the evening of September 27th 1946, a small single engine jet aircraft ascended rapidly into the sky above the De Havilland aircraft factory in Hatfield Hertfordshire, its destination was the Thames Estuary forty miles to the east. The aircraft was the De Havilland DH108 Swallow; an experimental aircraft intended to test new concepts in aircraft design. The DH108 represented the cutting edge in technology of the time when Britain, the United States and the Soviet Union were at the beginning of the fierce technological race of the Cold War.

The purpose of the flight on that late summer's day was to conduct a practice run in preparation for an air speed record attempt to be conducted later that year. The aircraft had already unofficially surpassed the air speed record of 616 mph, and it was intended to try for an officially recorded speed run over the official course at Tangmere in West Sussex.

The futuristic profile of the Swallow would surely have provided a magnificent spectacle. By the standards of the day, the streamlined tailless aircraft, with its swept back wings, must have looked truly impressive to onlookers below as it sped across the sky accompanied by the roar of its 3300 lb thrust turbo-jet engine. It was a new sound to be heard in the skies; it must have sounded much like an approaching storm to a population not yet familiar with the sounds of jet aircraft.

Test flying is a hazardous undertaking; in this profession disaster is not uncommon. Therefore, the isolated flatlands of the Thames Estuary would have provided a favourable location for such a test flight; the area was, as today, largely unpopulated. It was while flying at about 8000 feet at a speed of Mach 0.88, close to the speed of sound, that the aircraft broke up. Wreckage fell into the mud of Egypt Bay on the North Kent Marshes and the pilot, 36-year-old Geoffrey De Havilland Junior, was killed in the crash. A search ensued, and a Mosquito crew spotted the wreckage in the shallow water of Egypt Bay.

The Swallow. DH108 model made by Victor A. Tester 1950.

THE DE HAVILLAND DH108 SWALLOW
A RESEARCH AIRCRAFT.

The DH108 program was intended primarily to provide research into the swept wing design that was to be used for the DH 106 Comet and the DH 110 Sea Vixen. With the advent of jet-powered aircraft in the early 1940s, ever-higher air speeds were attained. One of the purposes of the DH108 program was to investigate the behaviour of aircraft at transonic speed. It was discovered that speeds close to the speed of sound, Mach numbers 0.71 to 1.2 termed transonic, presented a special set of problems for aircraft designers[α]. Furthermore, at the speeds encountered close to the speed of sound, Mach 1, the aerodynamic forces acting upon an aircraft are considerable.

The DH108 was essentially a DH100 Vampire fuselage, attached to which were the innovative wept wings. The aircraft were tailless with a vertical stabilising fin.

Work began on the DH 108 in October 1945; in all, three aircraft were constructed. The first DH108, TG283, flew in May 1946 under the control of Geoffrey De Havilland Junior. The first prototype was a low speed aircraft, capable of speeds of 280 mph. Its purpose was to investigate the flying characteristics of the swept wing design at low speeds. Its engine output was 3000 lb.

The second prototype, TG306, was intended for research at higher speeds with an engine output of 3300 lb. The aircraft first flew in August 1946, and it was this aircraft that crashed at Egypt Bay in September 1946.

The third prototype, VW120, had an engine output of 3750 lb, and first flew in July 1947. On September 9 1948 the aircraft exceeded a speed of Mach 1.0 in a dive between 40,000 and 30, 000 feet over the Windsor area, becoming the first purely turbo jet powered aircraft to officially exceed the speed of sound. The speed of sound had previously been exceeded officially by the rocket powered Bell X1 and the mixed powered Douglas Sky Rocket, both of the USA.

Sadly, all three DH 108 aircraft crashed killing their pilots. TG283 crashed on May 1st 1950 near Hartley Wintney Hants, and VW120 crashed on Feb 15 1950 near Birkhill Bucks.

EGYPT BAY, A PLACE IN OUR HISTORY

On a late summer's evening at the beginning of the 21st century, tranquillity prevails at Egypt Bay. It is remarkable to reflect that seven decades have now passed since a pioneer of our age travelled there on a mission of exploration, into the uncharted realms of the transonic, where he was to meet his fate. The vessels of an earlier age of exploration, which passed along that same river, took weeks or months to travel between continents. But in that new age of rapid technological progress, which the Swallow's striking aerodynamic profile personified, the wings that fell over Egypt Bay in September 1946 rapidly evolved. Within a few years the world had shrunk as the gulf between continents was reduced to hours. This quiet backwater of the Thames estuary has a small but significant part in the history of the exploration of a new realm at the dawn of a new age in exploration: that of high-speed aeronautics.

Vast and isolated: the final destination of TG306.
Photograph by Clive Tester 1989

DH108 SPECIFICATION, SECOND PROTOTYPE TG306.

- Wing sweepback: 45°
- Length: 24 ft 6in
- Engine: Goblin 3 turbojet engine. 3300 lb thrust.

ACKNOWLEDGMENTS FOR APPENDIX D

A special thanks is extended to Dr. Roger Simmonds and to Andrew Blackwell for the help that they have provided during the research for this appendix.

This appendix was prepared using the following information sources: -

- $^{\alpha}$At the Edge of Space by Milton Thompson, 1992. ISBN 1-56098-107-5
- Dr. Roger Simmonds, 2005.
- Andrew Blackwell, 2005.

- http://www.unrealaircraft.com/wings/dh108.php

- http://www.icarusbooks.com/hpm.htm

- http://www.csd.uwo.ca/~pettypi/elevon/gustin_military/db/br/DH108SWA.html

- http://www.channel4.com/science/microsites/S/speedmachines/soundbarrier_timeline_t.html

- http://www.neam.co.uk/vampire.html

- http://tanks45.tripod.com/Jets45/Histories/DH108/DH108.htm

- www.nationalarchives.gov.uk

Views from the 20th Century

The two images above show a pontoon crane on Cliffe Marshes in February 1964. One of the workers in these photographs is Cyril Edwards. Photograph courtesy of Andrea Kennard, daughter of Cyril Edwards.

The end of an era. The demolition of Quarry Cottages in 1985. The fireplace of Burt and Sis Hoare's home is on the left. Many of us hold dear memories of sitting by the glowing coals of this fireplace with a cup of tea and enjoying their kind hospitality. Photographs courtesy of Don and Ross Pople.

The pontoon crane on Higham Marshes photograph taken in 1991 by Clive Tester.

Quarry Cottages photographed from the Francis Chalk Quarry in the 1950s or early 1960s. Photograph by Albert Smith courtesy of Martyn Smith

Views from the 21st Century

The reed bed at the site of Ivy House. Clive Tester October 2015.

Spartina grass on the mud flats of Cliffe Creek. Clive Tester October 2015.

Printed in Great Britain
by Amazon